BUYING ONLINE

Newcastle Poetry Prize Anthology

2018

Buying Online: Newcastle Poetry Prize Anthology 2018

Published by
Hunter Writers Centre and the University of Newcastle
Newcastle NSW 2300

Email: publishing@hunterwriterscentre.org

Buying Online: Newcastle Poetry Prize Anthology 2018

22 21 20 19 18   1 2 3 4 5
ISBN-978-0-6484099-0-8(paperback)

Cover design by Gillian Humphries
Typesetting by HWC Publishing
2018 Published by Hunter Writers Centre Inc.

© Each poem is copyright of the respective author
© This collection copyright of Hunter Writers Centre

All rights reserved.
No part of this publication may be reproduced, stored in a retrieval system, or transmitted in any form by any means electronic, mechanical, photocopying, recording or otherwise without the prior consent of the publishers.

Table of Contents

–Winner Newcastle Poetry Prize
BUYING ONLINE — 2
Ross Gillett

– Equal Second Prize
Five Replies to Miss Moore — 6
John Watson

– Equal Second Prize
The River Running Shallow — 12
Mark Tredinnick

– Commended
Thirteen Ways of Knowing My Father — 16
Kevin Smith

– Commended
Time Travelling with Baby — 22
Joanne Ruppin

–Winner Harri Jones Memorial Prize for a poet under 35
The Memory of Snails — 23
Chloe Wilson

A disco in the bush — 28
Adam Gibson

Broken Door — 30
Darby Hudson

Tidal — 31
David Adès

unmothering — 36
Kristin Hannaford

Secession — 38
Guy Kelleher

Fractured States of America — 39
Maria Takolander

The War—Then and Now	44
Andy Kissane	
A Survey of Australia's Religions	51
Damen O'Brien	
Shackleton's Hut	54
Mark O'Flynn	
King Tide	58
Toby Fitch	
Operations	61
Andy Jackson	
The breadth of the moment	64
Kristen Lang	
Box Brownie Album	66
John Watson	
The Mill Road	72
Kevin Smith	
Desert flaneurs	75
K A Nelson	
Grief Wears a Body	78
Mark Tredinnick	
Driver	80
Vidhya Karnamadakala	
Equations for a Falling Body	82
Sarah Holland-Batt	
The Wee-Vee	87
B.R. Dionysius	
Wherever this is it's where we are	92
Alison Flett	
Versities: Building X	93
Peter Kirkpatrick	
The Reservoir	96
Mark Tredinnick	
Prepping for the Apocalypse	99
Robert H. F. Carver	
A Poem Containing Violence	102
Joan Fleming	
About the Newcastle Poetry Prize	122

Introduction

Judging a poetry competition of this scale is like tapping a vast aquifer; it offers a privileged insight into not always evident aspects of the society we live in. Michael Leunig once said of his cartoons: 'I must say out loud what people are whispering.' As we read through these many poems we had a similar sense of listening to what is going on behind the scenes in Australia. Ideas, opinions, reflections, experiences and stories are all evident in a collection of poems such as this; some people whisper, some shout out loud.

It's interesting to read the themes and preoccupations that emerge at this time in history, some of which are universal, some of which are particularly Australian and some that engage directly with the present day. Many of the poems submitted respond to the personal and private, many respond to the social, the public and the political, and also the historical. Many are clearly the work of a lifetime of dedication to reading and writing poetry in all its nuances; a number appear to be new to this art form. All have value in different ways. Many of the poems that didn't make it to the long list were poignant or capable of acute and memorable lines.

Our advice to those who are curious to learn more is to make sure the reader has a role in your poem. Avoid sermons and dissertations, they leave no room for the reader's imaginative response. Know when to stop. Numerous poems wrote to the maximum line length at cost to the integrity of the poem: less can be more. Sometimes, a gem of a short poem was embedded, agate-like, within a much longer poem. Plain words can be powerful. A tight, well-crafted short poem in our view is as equal a contender for a prize as any.

Finding the poems that rise to the surface can almost be equated with the writing act itself. It's a slog, which takes discipline, patience, a listening ear, and the application of a hard head and open heart. You have to live with and through the process, stepping away at times, sitting with certainties and doubts, then returning again to the decisions you have to make. Soon enough you recognise poems that won't let you go. Something about their insistent voice, their message, their logic, tone and imperative brings you back to them amid so many others.

Buying Online is such a piece, one that impressed us both on a first reading. Returning to it was always a pleasure. It begins . . .

> *If the hook arrives bent*
> *put it down to the curvature of the earth.*

From its opening lines it speaks with a controlled creative flair, in a manner that looks deceptively simple—a skill we know takes years to develop. The conceit of it—the place, function and hope of poetry in a wild world of chance, weather and commerce, made it a welcome delivery. It's understated in its wisdom and invitation, and being about the weight and heft of poetry in a material world, there is a palpable irony to it in the context of this competition.

> *Money heads for the horizon and disappears.*
> *It comes back*
> *as poetry.*
>
> *Such small amounts of money,*
> *so many poems*
> *responsive to the gravity of being in the world.*

Over the course of our reading we both became acutely aware of the '*so many poems/responsive to the gravity of being in the world*'. We were moved by the breadth of human responsiveness on display, the necessity of expressing joy, faith, doubt or profound grief through poetry. To see such a world of it, poem after poem, was a privilege neither of us will forget for some time. The two poems that we awarded joint runners up account for something of that range.

Five Replies to Miss Moore is a playful piece with impressive, imaginative force. Referring of course to the poet Marianne Moore, we are reminded of her famous line, poetry as 'imaginary gardens with real toads in them'. This poem is both acutely clever and comedic, balancing those qualities with a skillful drive all the way to the end. It's the kind of poem that makes you want to immediately return to the beginning and start over, rewarding you with each read.

> *We at Key West and other readers at Loch East*
> *applaud your attention*
> *to detail and oddity and/or quiddity, which allows*
> *the flash and shriek*
> *of six lorikeets swooping through she-oaks*
> *to be fully honoured.*

The River Running Shallow is a poem that's altogether different, and one that's deeply affecting. It speaks of the deep grief of a father for his children. This poem transforms profound grief and loss into words of wisdom, beauty and restraint. The containment of great personal tragedy into iambics and blank verse give this poem's form a weight to shoulder, something it manages with grace.

> *Grief is proof of love; it lets you walk*
> *"The sweet music of your particular heart"*
> *In step with all you thought you'd lost—but can't.*

Trying to separate these two completely compelling poems became such a complex task, that in all truth, the only decision we could arrive at was to award them equally. There are times when a recourse like this is both fitting and fair and these two works, toe to toe, deserve to share that platform.

Of the two commended entries, *Time Travelling with Baby*, is a finely tuned example of a villanelle. The cyclical form lends itself well to subjects in which linear progression of thought is not imperative, subjects which call for teasing out and reflection on an idea or theme without temporal development. It is a good form for driving a point home—playfully, seriously, humorously, melancholically; this poem about absence and distance brings all of these together.

13 Ways of Knowing my Father, it's title a time-honored nod to Wallace Stevens, immediately snaps the reader awake with its vivid imagery and disturbing scenes. It's a good example of how brevity and restraint provides depth and resonance to a poem, these portraits depicting not only a father but the ripple effects of his presence within the family.

We commend these poems to you, congratulating the winners and encouraging all entrants. Many thanks also to the Hunter Writers Centre for their support throughout the judging process and for the exposure and opportunity a prize like this offers to those who live by and through the poetic line.

Sarah Day and Nathan Curnow

Awards
2018 Newcastle Poetry Prize

First Prize
BUYING ONLINE
Ross Gillett

Equal Second Prize
Five Replies to Miss Moore
John Watson

Equal Second Prize
The River Running Shallow
Mark Tredinnick

Commended
Thirteen Ways of Knowing My Father
Kevin Smith

Commended
Time Travelling with Baby
Joanne Ruppin

Winner Harri Jones Memorial Prize for a poet under 35
The Memory of Snails
Chloe Wilson

THE UNIVERSITY OF
NEWCASTLE
AUSTRALIA

Winner 2018 Newcastle Poetry Prize
BUYING ONLINE
Ross Gillett

1

If the book arrives bent
put it down to the curve of the earth.

Money heads for the horizon and disappears.
It comes back
as poetry.

Such small amounts of money,
so many poems
responsive to the gravity of being in the world.

2

Our days are salt-stained.
They come to us from some hidden anchorage,
they have passed through the straits.

They bring us cargoes of time and light.
We are safe harbours for them.

Put everything on the line to send for them.
Risk your details,
trust your carrier,
order all the days you can afford.

3

There's the olive leaf concept,
the dove returning
with an image of the saved world.

It takes a whole branch to mean peace
but Noah was thankful for the immense small mercy.

How many love poems from the last century
does it take to save this one?
Send for them
and they fly in like fierce doves.

As for the raven who never returned,
who knows what poem he has become.

4

Remember the drowned poems.

Lost overboard
in the oceanic distances.

Wrecked in our famous gales.

Some washed up on the steep beaches
with their lifeless forms intact.

As they were buried
they were read.

All that truth legible at the edge of the grave.

5

Poetry can come by air,
trailing clouds of vapour.
Glory of a sort.

You pay more,
but the poems reach you at high speed
and their sound trails behind them.

Open the book,
pick a word
and brace yourself
for its full weight to land on you.

You will feel the breaking
of the meaning barrier.

6

Imagine a poem light years away,
moving at 186,000 miles per second.
It may take centuries to reach us.

If it has mass
the poem will be infinitely heavy.

We don't want it crashing into our minds
at the speed of light.
The weight of its words would be unbearable.

But the poem *is* light.
It will arrive
as a weightless wavelength of language.

None of us will live to read it.

It will threaten nothing.
It will change everything.

7

There's a stained poem.
Rain has damaged the book it belongs to.

The poem cannot be blamed for poor packaging
or rough handling,
but bad weather now needs to be read into it.

Dampness has reached up the page
and invaded the last stanza.
The poem's ending is underpinned by a vague warping.

Keep the book.
Forget a refund.
It's a bonus,
this poem open to the elements.

Think of the weather wanting to get to the poem,
the rain being interested enough.

8

If the book is badly bent
poems won't recover.

They will be haunted
by contortions.

They will never flatten.

They will be left with an undulation,
a lift in the lines
no one knows the meaning of.

9

These are spindrift words.
They hang back
from the main point.

They make the smallest possible impact.
They will come to nothing.
You can have them free of charge.

Feel their faint rain,
thoughts that fade as they hit you.

Equal Second Prize

Five Replies to Miss Moore
John Watson

Aloha and Alley-oops to you also
and may we say at the outset –
in our zoot suits –
that your cheetah-praising,
                         charming letter
requesting details of the bifurcating fig moth mother
and palindromic genomes, as recently sheeted home
in the Scientific American, came
at an opportune time.
                  In search of rhyme
Our composting staff have been sorting
                        through a scree
of archive boxes stacked in the conservatory
and overflowing into the clerestory,
largely and with largesse the recollections
of etymologists and entomologists
                              who at our Christmas party,
played Hunt the Slipper and endeavoured
to Pin the Tail on the Donkey
                     to celebrate
their discovery of several conjunctions of oddity.
These, they explained, at once and as one,
                       you would have liked.
And, incidentally, that moth which finds itself
                       in something of a spot,
the fig operculum or oculis being so tight
(*Oculis* : fig as Pantheon : Metaphor alert!)
                        bears out the old saw, *What
goes up may have difficulty coming down.*
And may I say too
that your choice of verse form
                        rang resounding chimes
amongst our resident atmospheric scientists
who liken your stanza entering the lists

'arbitrarily concocted in response to the material
       and then repeated forthwith'
to cloud drifts accompanying blue sky
until sunset when they reappear exactly.
      Now to your request:
we have forwarded separately under plain post
a venery of images including as a bouquet
dolphins surfing at dusk along the coast.
       In a previous letter you enthuse
and describe seeing at the movies
'one of the most beautiful things I've ever seen',
alligators in an Alabama alligator farm
        repeatedly labouring up a bluff
so as to slide down a chute into water.
This we take to exemplify the old saw, put roughly,
      what goes up with difficulty
may often come down with enjoyment.
      And now we, representing
the ancient Guild of Mermen, salute you with raised tridents.

      O

You note that although leopards
    have no spots
on their underfur, they are represented
    in illustrations
and Indian textiles as having them
    and that therefore
it is pleasing to give them spots there
    and on their toes
keeping the reader on his.
    Is this not an index
of what separates art and reality
    and further, of the broad
church and foreign field of contrivances
    such as Mr Pound
reports that you have confided in him,
    namely, the compositional principle
that the form of the opening stanza depends
    on the exigencies of the matter

after which every stanza exactly repeats that form?
We at Key West and other readers at Loch East
                applaud your attention
to detail and oddity and/or quiddity, which allows
                the flash and shriek
of six lorikeets swooping through she-oaks
                to be fully honoured.
And Ursula – she of the Migrating
                House Martin Support Team –
wishes to add her own endorsements via this letter,
                particularly of the pangolin,
asking me to say, 'I cannot think
                of that crescent creature
without thoughts of Miss Moore and her fantastical
                menagerie of syllables.'

                O

Like Gieseking playing Scarlatti!
Here is, let us be clear,
your most exemplary simile
because, of course, we do not

think of a specific likeness
and yet must have heard him play
and concur fervently, remembering
many instances of splendour.

Therefore we reply to your letter,
not only to agree with you
that, yes, 'a story
with its attendant spirit

a bona fide baby elephant'
would indeed be 'irresistible'
but to revisit that simile
and again nod assent,

celebrating Gieseking *and* Scarlatti
without being any closer

to its demonstrable point of application
despite universal enthusiasm.

Euphoria might lead us on,
citing your *katy-did wing*
for its particularity and transparency,
to mention a pansy vase we have filled

here and now with yellow (and other) pansies
like swimmers floating on their backs
their heads thrown back horizontally,
faces looking up at the sky.

O

What we admire – as much as anything –
is your capacity to turn to gold the least obliquity,
load every rift, or – having found such rifts
in, say, the *Scientific American* –
        gift wrap these as gifts.
Your twelve-page letter was remarkable
not least in its adventuresome metallurgies. And,
incidentally, Harry has the lurgies, but
sends his best selections from the Periodic Table,
insofar as he is able.
        A blaze of sunlight,
like a determined weft, has by afternoon
        reached the room where you slept.
Beatrice, a cousin you have not met,
        who collects butterflies
or, rather, pictures of them – nothing to be netted –
joins Mother in hoping you will write again
with that recipe of renown
        for charcoal biscuits, which,
before the Yankees thrashed the Brooklyn Dodgers,
that soldier wrote out for you on cigarette paper.
And if you write again, please include
the latest on cheetahs.

O

On the beach approaching dusk
                – how sweetly
the participle equivocates,
suggesting it was we who approached
along the seven miles' curve
                – a pleasing notion
since dusk might well be imagined
gathering itself there in the south –
And how well you have noted such vagaries
                which language generates,
shuffling from transitive to intransitive,
verb to adjective and back,
Chaucer's language still looking for a subjunctive…
              On the beach
were many kangaroos lying about
as if they were guardians,
arms too long to fold comfortably
with no-one else on the beach at all
other than these soft-elbowed lazing persons
in a sea wind, the air white with spray,
description written everywhere like scribble gums
              and a grey green headland
setting out to sea, and a star
            to steer her by.
There we were in the midst of language
and seaspray, not only not seeking a theme
and seeking it in vain,
            but in fact
studiously seeking to avoid a theme;
in fact to fly a windy sky of kites
along a deserted beach,
            each having
no connection with any others.
Now to lunge even further along that long beach
            of the past,
the true subject of almost every letter ever written:
the guest house where I stayed as a child
while my father waited for an official house –
and on whose verandah I rehearsed
            the multiplication tables
with my mother seeming to listen –

has long disappeared, the site now a forest;
The steep hill it looked down descends
                        without an audience.
Nearby a barking dog, cicadas like surf, bellbirds
and, in the large visual field, huge
jacarandas, silky oaks with yellow bracts
                        and gold-foil Robinias.
Here it was as a child that Language
threw its lariat round me in the line
                        (from Walter de la Mare)
and a bush, in the corner, of may
whose commas and dislocation even then
                        troubled me without remedy.
And how refreshing it might be
to come upon a young forest of objects
                        not yet assigned names
and without rules governing their interaction,
and to fire off a letter asking advice
                        about their management,
to which we wait your reply.

Equal Second Prize

The River Running Shallow
Mark Tredinnick

1.
Nothing the world was once so gifted at
Knows how to fill the silence that my children
Leave, gone missing from my days.
                                        Give
Yourself back to what you love, they say,
But all I give the sadness takes away. I try
To muscle up, building a body fit to bear
All that my mind cannot. My arms grow
Strong, my stomach taut, but who is there
Anywhere to hold and swing and play the fool
And lift high in the surf?
                         I try to love again,
But something in me cannot learn to yield
To love's insubordinate commands, and all delight's
Become a foreign currency that buys me
Nothing here.
              I used to learn fast, and I know
It's myself I need to study to understand,
My own life and what's inherent there
And adequate and entire. I score well at
The multi-choice of the examined life,
But when they want an essay, all that comes
To mind is every day I live a half-life
In the absence of my children's names.

2.
Dusk along the river knows nothing
About three children who never, so far, walked it
With me; the river running shallow way
Down deep in its four-storeyed banks is innocent
Of all three storeys of the house my mind
Bears on its back: my *grief* for the living,
Taught each day I'm dead to them, for days
I used to know with them, days died back
Like forest after fire on which the rain
Disdains to fall;
              the *violence* done to hope
Each day it wakes in them and rises in me
And tries to fly us back together again;
And down in the basement, the deep *despair* that floods
The circuitry that used to keep the lights on
Day and night, the chaos that corrodes
The chemistry the mind employed to make
Each minute mean a world.
                        I've lost the rhythm,
Misplaced the algorithm, that used to know
My way. But here outside myself, it seems,
A universe is being born, a place
That wants me in it.

3.
            Its innocence of me
And mine is what I take myself to the river
To find, when the heat of unrelenting days
Of summer begins to yield at dusk: the silence
The sheoaks and the bracken have no mind
To keep, the patience the creek's the master of
(The way it *is*, no matter what things seem),

The truth that is the only thing that it knows
How to tell. The river at dusk can keep
My cries and teach my feet and both my thighs
To carry me on until my silence one day
Spills again its banks.
                      Till then, the river
Is my Orpheus and I, its underworld.

4.
And by the fence the cattle crop the grass,
And in a rising easterly the sheoaks
Sing all distance into one lament,
And a wagtail raps a sweet farewell.
                              The wilding
Weather wants the blue shirt off my back,
And a whipbird, the sweetest dominatrix in
The world, sings her lash and elicits a cry,
A happy lullaby from her helpless, hapless
Mate. A working man, walking calm
His working dog, catches me, taking elicit
Pictures of the sky, and I walk with him
A mile and talk and find myself a man
Again, any other per-ambulant tenant
Of a place, a being on the earth.

5.
And at the bend a foretaste of the evening
Pools and wells, and I swim the scent of ages
Past, the learning way down deep in things,
And I feel a coolness like the dawn upon
My skin.
          The sky, meantime, premeditates
Some rain, which, as I turn, deigns to fall,
Desultory, a while, upon the descant
Chat of children after dinner, beyond
The hedge.

      And step by step my mind relents,
And night becomes a house where all I carry
Puts itself to bed—three children, tired
Now of being every sound that heard them
In my head, and every way they were not
Here, but were the rehabilitated
Sense the river running shallow in deep
Banks made of where I found myself,
Accompanied each step by all I love.
Before they sleep my children read me this:
Grief is proof of love; it lets you walk
"The sweet music of your particular heart"
In step with all you thought you'd lost—but can't.

NOTES
Grief is proof of love: I have in mind thoughts from Julian Barnes's *Levels of Life*.

"The sweet music of your particular heart": "Love allows us to walk/ in the sweet music of our particular heart"—Jack Gilbert, "The Great Fires."

way down deep in things: alludes to Gerard Manley Hopkins's "There lives the dearest freshness deep down things," from "God's Grandeur."

In step with all you thought you'd lost: I have in mind "That day I'll be in step with what escaped me," the closing line of Seamus Heaney's "Squarings xlviii."

Commended

Thirteen Ways of Knowing My Father
Kevin Smith

     1

The sheep snorted from the back
of the wagon. A clutch of legs roped
together jutted above the back
seat. Butcher's knife and steel
rattled in the footwell. The smell
of sacrifice seeped into
the upholstery as we pulled up under
the killing tree. A butcher's hook
hung above a bloodstained block.
Crows gathered in rags of mourning,
torn from the night. 'Come on', my father said.

     2

He was a minor disciple of Christ
far below a carpenter
in the scheme of creation. His vow of poverty
hammered us into a life of privation.

3

On the logging road far
above the mill he fell asleep
at the wheel of the white Falcon.
When it crashed into a mountain
ash the plonk bottle leapt off
the back seat and smacked into
the windscreen moments after my father's
head. He was full of grog
returning from a fishing trip
with an empty bucket and a busted rod.

4

The bandsaw sang as it carved a canyon
through my father's hand. A sticky
scrawl of blood on sawdust glistened
like icing on a cake. His red wound
sutured itself into my dreams.

5

We never knew our father's father.
When he died Dad disappeared
for a week. Mum said nothing as she hung
the washing. Us kids swapped looks
then went off hunting Snoopy Warner's
chooks with bows and arrows cut
from wattle saplings. Dad came back
quiet. That night we argued as usual
about who would do the washing up.

6

One of the workers died at the mill.
A log slipped from a winch and he
was pinched to death between two
giant trunks of alpine ash,
his head a red pustule about
to pop. A tree full of kooka-
burras rocked the log yard
with laughter. After, the men milled
around a fire drum in the snow,
disappeared one at a time
up to the office to talk to the coppers.
Before he was called my father stood
alone blowing into his hands.
That night at the kitchen table an apostle
of silence took its place among us.

7

Friday nights the white Falcon
lurched along the nine miles
of dirt road home. Behind
the wheel my father wrestled with
our fate, his drunkenness a merry-
go-round for our panic, his face a florid
slippery-dip in the dull glow
of the dash. 'Get over, Darl!' my mother
screamed again, and again, her face
contorted in the cracked side mirror
into a circus freak flushed
with horror. Somehow, the slug gun
marksman always got us home.

8

At 51 he lay in a hospital
bed chest broad and bare,
breath thin, tubes out his nose
a ring of children around him nailed
to their pain. He died anyway.

9

"This meat's off," my brother said.
My father exploded out of his chair
grabbed him by the throat and reefed
him from the table and flogged him hard
and long on the bare floorboards in front
of us all. The house held its breath.
My mother stared ahead, saw
the writing on the wall: too many
mouths to feed, a long-drop
dunny, three kids to a room,
the constant drip of poverty.

10

Us twins bounced across
the back seat of the Falcon as it trucked
and joggled up Back Creek Road.
The rumble of the engine filled the no-
man's-land of silence between
us and our father. "Why don't youse jump
over into the front?" he said.
Me and my brother looked at each other,

weighing up the dangers of being
invited into the inner circle.

    11

On fishing trips to the Murrumbidgee
we camped in the bush. Dad dropped
the double bed mattress off
the roof of the Falcon, set the radio
up on the bonnet and shot through.

Mum and the girls set up camp.
Us boys trawled the shallows for mussels.

Dad tackled the river, headed
downstream to search for the deep
shady holes. Away from the clamour
of the camp a transenna of silence closed
behind him. My father's faith lay
in setlines anchored to rough-barked
river gums. On an outcrop of bedrock
he settled into silent prayer
to a slippery god: the Murray cod.

    12

My father's buried in a dry cemetery
on the edge of a small country town.
Every five years or so
I go back, walk the stony
tracks between the headstones. His black
marble slab looms in full

sun. Like a giant hand
it slaps me back to childhood.
I'm seven again and small as a seed
on the long fall from my father the tree.

    13

One winter we played in the snow,
my father and his tribe of bastard
children. He'd grab one of us,
shove a snowball down our back
and we'd disappear inside to the fire.
I was the last one left. And I
laughed into the wind at the sheer
joy of having him to myself
at last.

Commended
Time Travelling with Baby
Joanne Ruppin

I play among the pixels in long-distance peek-a-boo
reaching through a southern sunrise to relay a kiss good night,
time travelling from my laptop. Smiling. Pining. Missing you.

Our words touch, caress the darkness, cradle morning with delight.
We're both yawning while you drift toward young dreams where I have been.
I'm reaching through my sunrise to relay your kiss goodnight.

Sunbeams romp with fading firelight around faces on a screen.
Weave your nursery rhyme with mine and feel our lullaby complete,
we're both yawning while you drift toward young dreams where I have been.

Cockatoos coat eucalypts with screams of shimmering white heat
while behind you pale snow wafting past a street light paints the night.
Weave your nursery rhyme with mine to feel our lullaby complete.

I call from your tomorrow and watch yesterday take flight.
In our cocoon somewhere between you beam me cuddles and we play
while behind you pale snow wafting past a street light paints the night.

One last song to hold a memory for your night and for my day.
In our cocoon somewhere between, know I love you, here me say
I play among the pixels in long-distance peek-a-boo
time travelling from my laptop. Smiling. Pining. Missing you.

Winner Harri Jones Memorial Prize for a poet under 35
The Memory of Snails
Chloe Wilson

> UCLA biologists report they have transferred a memory
> from one marine snail to another,
> creating an artificial memory.
> – UCLA news release

> I admit I see a lot of things in this snail.
> – Daniel Arasse

You are the recipient of a gift: now you can remember
the beginning. Not your own: not
your progenitors rolling around blissfully
on some dewy lawn
on which they were surely trespassers
glistening and moonlit

not those days when you were essentially jelly –
not how you made your shell
by eating the egg you burst from, first,
then any siblings dim enough
to remain unhatched

and, once the rivals were dispatched
commencing your kindergarten découpage
layers and lacquer,
allowing your armour to harden

no, before that, before Hesiod said
he knew it was the harvest season
when we climbed the wheat

that's how we were named you know –
for that vulgar habit of walking as we eat
our kingdom is little more
than a a portmanteau: the word for stomach
the word for feet –

no, further back, a time before harvests, before
names – remember the ocean
its abyssal halls
where they left the lights off
to disguise the residents
their frightful overbites, the sloping noses
oblivious to the golden ratio. Before
we were both pest and delicacy. Remember

the paleolithic era, when everyone
developed a mania for protein,
remember becoming edible
remember the smell of our roasting shells
how we popped in the charcoal
how the viscoelastic fluid
sputtered and hissed

remember the Romans feeding us
until we were too fat
to retreat,
remember the legionnaires munching
as they made their dull march into Gaul

remember when we were reclassified
as fish
so our consumption could continue
unabated during Lent

without adding to anyone's teetering stack
of venial sins

remember how swiftly the sauté pan
conducted heat. Remember the seventy-two
of our number
swallowed by a bearded man
in three minutes flat.
He called it sport. You will remember
how he died

from indigestion. You'll be pleased
to recollect how we've enjoyed our
little vengeances, massing

    on the coast of Argentina, or razing one crop
after another, or
   hitching a lift on a marble balustrade
to some country pile in Buckinghamshire

   where we're still invading –
where we've almost made it from the garden
to the gate.

   Remember how it felt, all that salt
on your back. Remember the phenomenon
    known as osmosis. Remember metaldehyde. Remember
Sluggo, Corry's, Blitzem – how they sweetened
    the pellets with apple and molasses.

Remember, we were never the aggressor.

   Remember, even in the psalters
    where we make frequent cameos
as marginalia, it's the knights who charge at us –
   coming with lance and horse
    lumbering with all their spectacular regalia

   in our direction, remember the head-scratching
of scholars, later, finding so many of us among
the monks' usual complaints
  ah, my hand!
  this ink is weak!
    dandruff falls in the theologian's office
   sizzles like a martyr on the bar heater

Remember our likeness appearing in egg tempera
   remember del Cossa
     remember proto-photobombing the annunciation
  Remember we were a footnote
   in Crivelli's all-star altarpiece,
  Saint Francis humble-bragging
     about his sandals
   Saint Sebastian's permed insouciance

   and remember Matisse
wielding scissors in his sickbed

                              at one of Nice's gauche hotels
            his assistant
            snatching squares of coloured paper
                        out of the air
                        before they could escape
in the balmy resort breeze
                              remember becoming an abstraction
                                    in gouache

Remember Heracles, or better
            to say remember his terrier – who bit into one of us
                        on some grecian beach
                        his lips were stained

the rare, rich colour of the venom
                  we shoot into the eyes of predators

                  Remember each quarter-million of us
required to make a single gram of that dye
            Remember the vats outside of Tyre
                        far outside, because the stench
of our decomposition
                              was unbearable

            Remember Pliny the elder
            saying the colour was best
                              when it resembled clotted blood
            Remember Caesar's regal toga
in homage to Cleopatra, remember

            they knew the Earl of Surrey
            was a traitor because he draped himself
in that colour, it meant power, it meant
                                    triumph
                        it meant a plot –

            Remember later associations,
Remember the woman
            who came to Jung complaining
            she dreamed of us
                        dreamed of our slime, tacky like glucose
coating a tree. He handed her a plate, a knife and fork,

said help yourself –
the brainless, he believed, must be assimilated –

Remember riding on that head of lettuce
in the writer's giant handbag,
we were the one hundred companions
she brought to avoid that English delicacy
small-talk

Remember we've been a remedy for almost anything
any pox or cramp, any fever,
croup or pneumonia,
we've been left to ferment in donkey milk,
soaked in sodium chloride,
made into pastes, ointments, syrups
mints, chocolate pastilles
we are a strong anaesthetic
we bring brilliance to the skin.

Most recently there's been the experiments:
remember they delivered
a series of electric shocks
not painful, they said, just enough
to trigger a defensive contraction
we coiled up into ourselves
over and over

with each shock we'd take longer to unfurl
and you weren't there
but you remember,
you cannot relax either
you hold your breath

because you remember
because now you'll remember
forever. How did it all come back? Tell us.
Was it gradual like a cloud of violet ink
clearing underwater
or was the return sudden:
the judder of that electric shock –
a stiletto through the shell.

A disco in the bush

Adam Gibson

[Parnngurr, W.A. 9pm]

There's a big mob
gathered in from Punmu
and Jigalong, east from Warakurna,
over from Kunawarratji and
up from Parnpajinya, here for the funeral,
having arrived in battered cars
that you can't believe survived that road
and dust-sprayed Toyotas
that now sit like emperors
in the hot late-July sun.

The red dirt is rusted,
no shade beneath the trees with
all the lower branches
ripped off for firewood and
dogs fight amongst each other
as the service is conducted
on the red flat earth
in the centre of community.

Then night falls
and the kids emerge, creeping out
to the sound of music
pumping from DJ decks
in the community hall,
the new supply shop operator
spinning the tracks, he's cool,
while torches are flashed
in the dusty darkness and
dozens of faces line the walls.

The brave ones occasionally dart out to
show their best moves
- American hip-hop,
busts of rap and breakdance -
and then dart back again
when the attention turns to them too much.

The sound is of shouting and
the hum above the music of
massed laughter,
squeals of smiles and
the slap of bare feet
hitting bare floor
in a syncopation
that is rarely reported on the
evening news of the world
or in the telegraphs which herald
the important things you need to know.

Then, on the dot of 9pm,
the DJ plays his final song
and wraps it up with little fanfare,
the kids, without a grumble,
file out in an urgent rush,
disappearing in a dancing mob
towards their houses and camps
by the fires of 44 gallon drums
and dogs barking and fighting
beneath a sky in which
the Milky Way shines
with a bright buzzing light
you can still hear.

Broken Door

Darby Hudson

Despite my dad being an engineer,
I am not practical: I cannot
fix a broken door.

Instead, it opens and
invites the possibility for me to
write a poem about the door's
brokenness – how it
made me feel.

And yet as I sit here writing about
the broken door and my
unhandy-man feelings -
it's strange to
find I've inherited my
father's handwriting;
that movement is passed-down as
measured by pen or pencil.
And even more
uncanny: the curious bastardisation of
my father's font forming my
mother's crazy thoughts
across the page.

I've realised I only
need a small amount of
trouble to set a
poem alight.

Tidal
David Adès

Now I am an endless swimming
                in the restless seas of my children,

my muscles a constant burn and ache

keeping my head above the sparkle and glimmer and depths of them,
buffeted
      by chop and swell, by wave after wave after wave,
               by the vast oceans of their needs.

I could drift, inert, like seaweed,
                but I must mediate the tug and pull
of their cross-currents,
watch the line of one daughter's spine,
                the shift of her shoulder-blades
as she sits on a piano stool spooling out notes,
apprehend the toddler
            as he tears around the house on some manic mission
toothy-grinned and wicked with laughter,
contend with another daughter's
              relentless testing of boundaries.

Always, I watch for sharks and blood.

For so long
      I have forgotten my needs except in tossing dreams in turn forgotten,
the fog of forgetting swirling thick

but there is no shame in conjuring them:
                         I need an island to beach myself upon,
the luxury of sand, palm trees, coconuts, a cold mango lassi

and a woman with open arms, a welcoming smile,
                                  the invitation of her skin.

So much for dreams: the waves have me in their grip and I must swim on or sink.

Sometimes there are rhythms amid the turbulence,
the rhythm of a child's breath in sleep,
                   the rhythm of school days when no one is sick
and nothing is forgotten, when routines click into place
without sudden squalls,
            lashings of rain, howling winds
though nothing is given, the seas' blue calm never more than mere interlude.

I take whatever interludes I get,

hauling myself onto some shore
                          to scratch a few words in the sand
only to watch them erased by the incoming tide.

In Darwin,
        after the Mangrove boardwalk, where the girls took turns
in the hot sun reading signs
telling the story of the mangroves,
                      they walked on the beach, found pieces of coral
and shells, oceans to put to their ears,
and numerous holes in the sand,
                a living world at their feet.

The school principal
        declined applications for certificates of extended leave
deeming a week away from school
                  not to be within the girls' best educational interests:
and we are stuck
        with such a narrow definition of educational interests,
                                such obliviousness
and all it portends – the world at large
                providing nothing educational —

not the mangroves or the beach,
not the knowledge of the mangroves shared by the First Peoples,

not the two hours they both spent intently peering through microscopes
                                  in the Discovery Centre at the Museum
and making elaborate drawings
                      of sunflower pollen, hemp fibre, bottlebrush spore, cotton
fibre, fern spore, sponge gourd, common red sponge, wool, angora rabbit hair, mouse fur,
cat hair, camellia leaf section, bamboo shoot, leaf of aelium, pine wood, stem of corn, nylon,
onion rind, bemberg, pollen of lily,

not the rest of the day spent wandering through the Museum,
not the documentary of Aboriginal elders telling stories of their art,

not the exhibition of Aboriginal Art,
not standing before an artistic rendition of Maralinga
                    with all colour leached out and areas of smudged black and grey
and my explanation of the nuclear tests, the displacement and dispossession,
the blithe dismissal of culture,

not the wind-howling simulation of Cyclone Tracy,
not the photographs of Darwin's destruction,

not the entire world beyond the classroom, the schoolyard —

so that even as I lay down rules,
                          as I set boundaries,
as father, as guardian, as shepherd of safety,

I am willing the breaking of them, the breaking through,
I secretly cheer the testing, the challenging,
                          constant and inevitable as the back and forth
of the tides,
as I navigate fatigue and childhood,

as I beach myself each night

while three worlds make themselves
whether I can keep up or not.

unmothering
Kristin Hannaford

'This is what I have made of it. This!
…What, indeed?' Virginia Woolf, *Mrs Dalloway*

If you stand in front of a glacier
you will hear it pop and groan
as it grinds over the stratum of rocks beneath.
Moving at *glacial speed* it is quicker
than both you and I can imagine.
Great shards of ice calving
before its advance.

My sons have been leaving me my whole life.
In pieces, like fragments of ice or retina –
they have been slipping from my vision,
like words I can no longer read.
They walk before me into the long days
of adulthood; they do not turn.

I remember women talking.
Mothers. We dreamt of our children
as small and hungry parasites.
H. R. Giger aliens writhing within,
taking our teeth, hair and our bones.
Most days, we gave them up willingly.
Surrendered them to the garden,
to places outside.

Now, I am unmothering,
I would curl them back into me.
My imperfect, beautiful sons.

On the topic of global warming
and glacial retreat, the women are silent.
We are all watching my young men,
now model citizens before the state,
as they bend to secure crampons and tie laces.

And in the hours of their mistakes
I no longer know when to speak,
when to be silent,
or if they can hear
the screams in my head,
the desperate hours
as they walk ahead.

If you stand in front of the glacier
you can hear it pop and groan.
It is the sound of great canyons
and fissures opening between us.

Secession

Guy Kelleher

Broken down at park bench negotiations,
I ask what it would take to keep you in the Union.
Our stories entwined -
those of two proud peoples with a shared history.
A home, and a way of kissing.

Take your autonomy, guard your identity,
but please respect our Constitution.
This little nation has fought enough wars to get where we are!
The promise of some revolutionary new order fermenting in your conscience;
murmurings of a coup in a phone call to a friend.

So I've called this summit down by the river -
urging for caution, pleading for dialogue,
biting my tongue as any good diplomat should:
listening.

But your voice is softer than the movement of the water:
this is how I know
soldiers are already at the border.

Fractured States of America

Maria Takolander

1. Space Junk

God knows, the heavens had delivered all manner of disasters
to the upstanding people of Tulsa, Oklahoma:
deluges, tornadoes. Now what?
Searing the city skyline, after midnight,
this sphere of flame in cherry, sapphire, stunning white.
It reminded Lottie of the compact and righteous fury
of the Good Lord, but also (if she was honest)
high-school experiments with Bunsen burners.
Lottie was Baptist, but no creationist.
As she watched from her kitchen window,
        she felt there was a lesson in the fireball's silence.

When one blazing light became two, Lottie wondered
if she might be witnessing a star birthing.
Then the skyscrapers blocked her view.
Pragmatic about her health—her body was like a dog that needed
regular walking (regardless of her irregular hours at work)—
she laced her trainers and headed down the hall before she paused,
recalling her grandmother's account of the Race Massacre of 1921.
The national guard had bombed Black Wall Street (as it was called)
with homespun turpentine bombs, destroying 35 blocks of
businesses and family dwellings, killing hundreds.
        It had not made it into the history books at school.

Lottie remembered how some of the mysteries of the New Testament
were forbidden. The First Apocalypse of James
had been found in an Egyptian dump, scattered with tax receipts
and bills of sale for donkeys, all scrawled on papyrus.
She locked the door and took to the city outside,
which was so polluted by artificial light

that respecting the traditional order of day and night
seemed a pointless ritual. She wondered what it meant
for a star to be dividing. Perhaps conquering?
The Creek Tribe had named this place Tallasi,
        before it became the Oil Capital of the World.

Lottie knew many things, but what she did not know was this:
a Delta II rocket, having thrust
a military satellite into low-Earth orbit, was falling.
The plan: covert reabsorption into atmosphere.
Yet here it was, reveling in the exotic chemistry of heat,
shapeshifting in the lusty throes of transubstantiation—
until it hit a cold snap
and a piece of fuel tank was haphazardly trapped
in an organic shape: a leaf, the colour of ash.
It drifted (naturally) towards a stand of oak trees where
        it glanced off the fabric of Lottie's back.

Later, she was told the chances were one in a trillion.
Let the mathematicians fuss over calculations; she knew
that only a miracle had spared her
from the 250-kilogram mutant propellant chamber recovered in Texas.
She had been touched in the dark with such tenderness,
though when she interrogated the object with her fingernail,
it pinged like steel.
She remembered the story of Chicken Little.
How she longed for the city to wake up.
Come dawn, she took her piece of sky to the municipal library
        for cross-referencing against a history of revelations.

2. Sinkhole Alley

Jeffrey was sleeping in Tampa, Florida, when the land disappeared,
    abducting him and his second-hand bed.

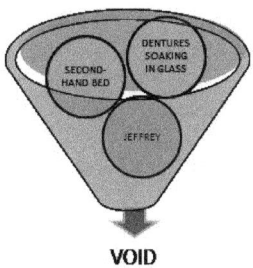

Emergency services quickened to the alien pit
    rimmed with torn ground-slab concrete, ragged fibro,

and hairy plaster bits. The hole was deep.
    They lowered in a listening device, but not one word

came from down below. "A piece of me,"
    Jeffrey's brother told the Tampa Bay Times, "is gone."

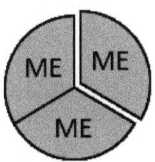

The engineers poured in low-slump aggregate grout,
    a freelancer released a camera drone,

and the authorities roped off the scene.
    The insurers, robbed even of breath by such

collapses of the firmament, had nothing to give.
>   The situation had become so unbalanced.

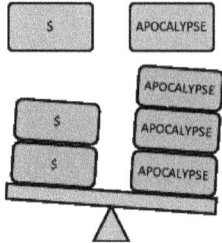

The world itself was now more of a threat
>   than terrorists. It obeyed no code of ethics.

It even stole from the retired, leaving funereal holes
>   in their manicured lawns.

In the trailer park, a young mother of six said the disappearing
>   reminded her of giving birth, only in reverse.

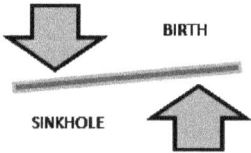

The Earth is reeling. Who would have thought
>   Mother Nature could do this to us?

3. Iceberg Wrangler

Yes, ma'am, I can tell you that more and more of these mammoths
are calving from Greenland and moseying
down past Newfoundland on the Labrador current,
creating all-mighty havoc in the North Atlantic shipping lanes.
Who will ever forget the *Titanic*? And the shrimp trawler
BCM Atlantic that sank in five minutes just last year?
My heart may be in Arkansas but I know that God needs me
right here, protecting the good men and women
of the Hibernia platform, drilling for crude in wild ocean,
with Storm Petrels crashing their lights and flare stacks.
These fine people risk everything
so that we can enjoy the great American life.
My daddy raised me on horseback and 100 acres of black cattle.
Riding on the *Norseman* (4,600 ton with a steel-reinforced hull),
I take lengths of polypropylene 1,200 feet long—and yahoo!
That rope starts out eight inches thick and comes back
gnawed as if by a hungry camel.
These free-roaming bergs can be the size of football fields
so if one bucks or kicks . . . Well, you have to be real careful
and slow. We tow at 1 knot or so.
My daddy always said to remember that I have a greater power
of understanding. And now I know
exactly when these rogues are close to breaking,
because they make a noise—they call it the Bergie Seltzer.
It sounds like a basket of chicken
sinking into an oceanic vat of oil.

The War—Then and Now
Andy Kissane

"You can tell a true war story by the way it never seems to end." —Tim O'Brien

All You Know

Crouching in the belly of the beast it smells bad—
gasoline fumes, sweat, the fear coming off
your skin. You have always been afraid of heights,
so it is some consolation to be strapped
to the metal ribcage of this raptor as it flies
over coconut groves and flooded rice paddies.
The Huey lands safely in a field beside a road—
deserted—and you head north-east, low hills
at your back, the sky a concrete grey pressing down.
A jumbled, wooden mess that was once a bridge
floats in the Sui Da Bang River, a squealing pig scurries
past a burnt out hut, an old woman stares as you pass
and you are not sure if you're despised or desired.
An hour later, you wade through the knee-high
ferns of a rubber plantation, the trees spaced
out as symmetrically as marching soldiers.
Thumbs down, a warning shout and you dive
forward, rifle ready, just as the sky collapses
with monsoonal urgency, the water sluicing
over your hootchie in frantic streams—then
white light, thunder. Des appears and tells you
to recce up ahead and see if Charlie's out there.
Like the day you played football in a hailstorm,
you run with your forearm shielding your face,
but if the enemy's about, you cannot find them.
That's all you know. Soon darkness slides
over everyone and the word comes through
that Dave's been hit and hasn't made it.
The rain stops as suddenly as it started.
You are numb, scared, thirsty. You listen
to the night, to the staccato rhythm
of water dripping onto the red, sodden earth.

The Mathematics of War

At school, I tried to follow Butch's explanations
of calculus and trigonometry, but his penetrating stare
and the aura of his shining head and bristling eyebrows
often left me immobilized with fear, sheltering
behind my desk. I had watched him punch boys
for not paying attention, for failing tests,
for uncompleted homework, I had watched his sudden
right cross strike for reasons I did not understand.
I didn't know then about the mathematics of war—
how we would set up our ambushes in the shape of a triangle
with two machine guns at the points of the base,
in a line that ran parallel to the killing ground,
the third gun trained on the connecting track
so we covered the entrances and exits, and later
could calculate the probable and confirmed body count
as if they were merely numbers chalked on a blackboard.

As the sun sinks below the orderly rows of rubber trees
and the stars from distant galaxies glimmer,
I recall how Pythagoras discovered that the consonance
and dissonance floating out of a blacksmith's forge
depended on the weight ratio of the hammers striking
an anvil. He believed that the orbits of heavenly bodies
produced a celestial hum that we cannot hear,
but might describe with the right equation. Glancing
at the harmonious moon, I break open my M79,
load the shell and raise the leaf sight so I can focus
on a range of three hundred and seventy-five metres,
where the explosion will kill everyone who would fit
comfortably into a typical classroom. I wonder if I
could graph the projectile motion of the tracer bullets
that will soon fly from my Slaughtermatic at a rate
of seven hundred revs a minute, with a muzzle velocity
of eight hundred and fifty-three metres a second.

But the problem is too hard for my exhausted mind.
Instead, I wait for men and women dressed in black
to run into a zone whose existence is unknown to them.
Personally, I'd want more than a probable survival rate
of zero over zero, an indeterminate expression that depends
on the pressure I apply to the trigger. What if I don't act?
Will I slip over to the other side of the equation? Become
as cold and bloodless as a statistic? I am not a machine,
even though they've trained me to kill like one.
As Butch might have predicted, I have never excelled
at mathematics or war. What hope do I have
of finding a solution? I draw a line in the dirt
with the tip of my index finger. Particles of dust
cling to my pink fingernail like unborn children.

The Firefight

You don't remember much
afterwards. You don't want to.
Though you dream it over
and over again—waking
under a sheet you've twisted
around your sweating body
as the sound of rapid fire
bludgeons the night & green
tracers fly about like some kind
of phosphorescent plague.
You hear a man scream obscenities
& another voice shout orders
with the same plosive panic
that has entered your bloodstream.
You feel the recoil dig
into your shoulder like shock,
glimpse the brilliant yellow flash,
a Catherine Wheel exploding
out of the grey palings of the back fence.
Des appears beside you, his thumb
hauling you in the direction of safety.
You hoist your pack & crabwalk
after him, before a monsoon
of mortar shells drops right there—
on the piece of dirt where you were
lying ... though in your dream
you are stricken, petrified, legless—
unable to run or crawl or do anything
to escape the barrage raining down
on you, night after sleepless night.

Jumping Jack Flash

A limp breeze from the north.
A waterbird lifts from the mangroves. I watch
until the glare of the sun makes me look away.
A stand of bamboo shifts in the heat haze.
Behind it, the village we will soon cordon and search.
Those dark frightened eyes staring at us.
We walk along this dry creek bed. Suddenly
I glimpse a white flash up ahead, hear
the boom and I know that someone has stepped
on a mine. His right leg, long strips of flesh
hanging off it, as if he's been flensed.
His left foot is not there, it's nowhere.
His left thigh grated, minced, covered in blood.
So much blood. It's Barnesy—face white,
a hole above his belt the size of a football.
The effortless spawn of a jumping jack.
Boffa calls for Des to come quick,
but it's too late. There's nothing to do.
He's my friend and there's nothing
to do. I don't pick up my Slaughtermatic,
dash into the village and blaze away.
I feel nothing. I sit down in this
blasted land while they call for dustoff.
The flesh hanging off his legs in strips.

Under the Bed

After Barnesy has been wrapped tight
in his hootchie and dusted off, we enter
this village whose name no one seems to know.
Yelling loudly, we move from house to house,
gathering the old, the women, the babies,
the children too young to fight, the men
who are not working in the fields.
We herd them into a makeshift holding pen
until they are pressed up against each other,
like cattle. Then we separate the men
of fighting age, as one might pick out
stones from a clay pot full of rice.

We make them squat with their legs open,
so our South Vietnamese interrogators
can kick and pummel their wedding tackle
until they give the required answers—
the location of tunnel entrances, the whereabouts
of Viet Cong leaders, the names of anyone
who feeds and harbours the enemy.

On a second sweep of the houses, I follow
Boffa into a room which holds a double bed
and not much else. He senses something, some
slight movement under the bed and he's firing
his submachine gun up and down the length
of the mattress, emptying the whole
cartridge, until the bed takes on the semblance
of a rattan screen and blood slowly
slides out and seeps down into the earth.

I can't really describe what concentrated fire
at close range does to a body—the mangled
faces, the sudden stink of lacerated organs,
the masses of blood, the horror, the horror …
When we pull them out from their hiding place
we discover that they are not armed—two men
about the same age as us, who were probably
just confused, frightened, hoping to stay alive.
Boffa looks at me and I respond with a nod
and we seal a contract to keep quiet and say

nothing. One after the other, we drag the men
by their ankles and lay them down
beside the drainage ditch that runs along the street.

What I see next I have no desire to remember,
but cannot easily forget—how one woman
screams, ducks under the white tape and runs
towards her husband? her lover?—until she is
stopped by a rifle butt crunching into her chest,
slips, falls and stays down in the dirt, crying.

I have no desire to remember how
she peers up at me from the ground, her pain
burning like an accusation laid out
before the whole village, before all of us—
men, women and children—who have watched this
and cannot do a thing to prevent or explain
or rescind what has just happened
and will never be mentioned in the official
dispatches to the generals and others
who are concerned with the conduct of the war.

A Survey of Australia's Religions
Damen O'Brien

Thirty per cent of Australians indicated they had no religion
– Australian Bureau of Statistics

      but we have saints taking Selfies, photo-shopping in halos,
or proselytising on the blogosphere, defending moral positions
with Emojis, their articles of faith with unfriending, texting psalms
and chants and hymns of praise, diet tips and cat photos;

      and there is worship in the reeling of a barramundi.
Sun God and sacrifice, brandished and measured
and every Sunday, burnt offerings send their smoke to heaven
from Webbers and from Bunning's best bargains;

      the ecstatic possession of holy fools rolling their eyes
outside a Saturday-night RSL, punch drunk and brawling,
king hits and confessions, pouring bitter into gutters,
sloshing sneakers and the scuffed floors of paddy wagons;

      you have your churches, Australia:
bright cathedrals roaring at each goal, heads bowed
in solemn hope of miracles, 20 points down, five minutes
to go, down by the Yarra, rained on at the Gabba;

      all the sacraments most precious, dispensed at
ten to eight and half past nine, at the Human Bean, the
Black Market, the Steam Room and the Mug,
transmuting manna at $5 a cup, 50 cents for soy;

      the Houses in their rites and disputation,
introducing defamation under Parliamentary Privilege to
the greater glory of God, ecumenical or schismatic in Bennelong,
tearing down false idols in bellwethers;

      we are not bereft of devotion, we are
downloading the thousand names of God via Google Film,
giving praise to Netflix, taking in vain House of Cards,
counting blasphemies through the seasons of Game of Thrones;

       the hollow stations of our pity:
third in OECD averages for charity at home, blowing out
for disasters and plagues overseas, our angels walk the same
streets as angels everywhere, asking *are you all right?*

       abandoning the pews for sticky bus-stops,
pressed wet-grass parks, backbone and heel prints on damp dunes.
Oh the observances on all the edges of this land! Plunging
into the mystery of the waves, each day riding the ineffable into the
beach;

       come wash your souls, come be shriven, where men
can beat their wives in the inviolable altars of their bedrooms, and
for zealots with gang tattoos and motorbikes, in the overflowing barbwire
Eden of Goulburn, no sinner cast out, no penitent forgiven;

       the broken providence of the desert, the defiled chapels
of the bush, we pay our respects to elders past and present,
chroming on the fast track to God under each overpass, generations
of despair, paying credit on their crosses with welfare cards;

       I am too full of God for the Productivity Commission,
too empty for the Unions, I have tithed to the ATO
and given freely to the Day Care Centres, I have stood
with the faithful in the queue, I have given unto Caesar what is Caesar's;

       revile the heathens for they produce
no takeaway cuisine to brighten our polity, for they have
tried to enter heaven by boat, let the heretics
be sent to Manus, or exchanged for fanatics out of Bankstown;

       cant and spirituality, madrassas and yeshivas
for all: the Telegraph, the Herald, the Financial Review intone
victimhood, elitism, left, right, do-gooders and political correctness,
nothing can be said, everything is permitted;

      Jedi believers in the Force are up, extolling
the virtues of light sabres in chat rooms, Wiccans down,
but the Messiah from Bowral has not yet returned and we
wait, staring at dead reefs and cleared forests for the end of days;

      there is much faith here, brother, but little belief:
the coal fired bishops, the steel refining cardinals, cattle popes.
We have much to be thankful for, much to praise:
a God for every voter, a ceremony for every day.

Shackleton's Hut

Mark O'Flynn

The inside of the hut was not long in being fully furnished and a great change it was from the bare shell of our first days of occupancy.
                                        Ernest Shackleton, 1908

Within the wooden hut the frozen ghosts remain.
The spectre of each image lurks in the memory
of a shadow, behind a door, just out of sight.
Consider these populated silences.
Not even dust settles among the socks,
which might be granite socks, hanging year
after year as though pegged in a catacomb.

The cupboards, made of packing crates, hold nothing more
than the chill of gleeful abandonment.
Not an insect stirs, nor interrupts.
Examine if you will the mausoleum of the bunks
their cold blankets like the hides of strange carcasses.
An icy hawser entwined about itself, the slowly growing
greying whiskers of the rope, left alone these hundred
years like a Grandmother's fossilised plait,
unmoved from where the last hand dropped it.

Beyond the stony beach the waves freeze mid
splash, the cliffs like bitten coconut,
and in the distance, sounding like a crepitating
gin & tonic in a long glass,
the Big Pav.
We are more concerned for the minutiae of wood,
the planks clinging to their weeping nails.
Even a gnarled crucifix with its bunions and knots,
wired to a shivering rock, is barely enough to divide
the ocean from the sky.
Not a single person but for his echo.

Dirty ice they call this melting slush,
or is it the slowly freezing sheet of sea
cohering to its own repetition.
Brr, that water looks cold.

Look at that microcosm's patch of snow,
those nail holes stopped in time, or else the peppered
expanse from east to west across the bare horizon
where no rescue comes galloping.

Where did the timbers come from that built this hut
to keep the emptiness at bay?
Who cooked? Who swept the floors?
From a wire line a pair of torn pants still hangs as though
waiting for their owner to return with a darning needle.
The axe marks in the boards where once a walrus,
sundered for the evening stew, bled out.
What might have been that vision
drowned in hunger and sorrow?
A butcher with an axe and a job to do.
> *Oh the whisky, the poor whisky*
> *lost at the bottom of the iced-over sea.*

On the distant side of Pony Lake the muttering penguins
stand about like onlookers at an accident,
perhaps the sinking of a ship through ice,
waiting for the cops to move them on.
In leaning light the tinned stuff of survival sits
rusted to the shelves, ephemeral and eternal as one.
Everywhere you look:
> *Irish Brawn,*
> *W. P. Hartley's Red Plum*
> *Bottled Pickles Liquid*
> *Aberdeen Marrow Fat,*
> *Sweet Midget Gherkins*
> *Moir's Red Currants,*
> *Fry's Concentrated Cocoa*
> *Henry Tate & Sons Sugar Cubes*
> *Toothpowder Entirely Free From Injurious Acids.*

A hot meal every evening,
the fire not permitted to go out.
All the makeshift shelving, neat
and tidy against the nightly blizzard's onslaught.
Also:
reams of mouldering paper for the first Antarctic novel.
Why else bring the printing press,

rich with jettisoned metaphor?
Bamboo snow shoes for the ponies,
like coiled hotplates on the Columbian stove.
The freshly washed braid of a fraying cable.
Man's best friend, otherwise known
as his hot water bottle, hanging on the back of a warped
door, while outside, still tethered to its stake
beside the empty kennels, white and scoured as ivory,
one of the dogs gives up its ribs to the wind.

Each shadow a frozen moment,
not even death has thawed them out,
those specimens mummified with cold.
Count them: 24 porcelain insulators –
like a string of teeth around a cannibal's neck.
Crystal spheres of pipettes in the lab
busy with fairies of ice, a chemical residue
in each, a dream's spark imagined
in apprehended bubbles of flight.

A chair wrapped in Hessian sacking to keep its shoulders warm.
The twisted mess of the first bicycle too fragile for its mission.
A petrified shaving brush for those who recall the empire.
King Edward and his Queen still hanging from a wall,
the toasts ever-ringing in the air with the clink of metal mugs.
    Oh the whisky, the poor whisky
    lost at the bottom of the cold cold sea.

Look: a roll of gauze bandage, itself a sepia wound.
Coiled serpent of the enema bag.
A patch of mould on a canvas tarpaulin
like the fur of a dead marsupial.
A box of broken eggs. A pair
of copper-ringed cuff-links like simultaneous sides of the moon.
Who'd need cuff-links in a place like this?
The leopard spots of rust on a shovel's silent face.
The loneliness of a safety pin.
Everywhere you look
each window an oblique glimpse of light
devoid of conversation.
Outside the great sugared continent

stretching away as far as it is possible to go
in time and distance on ski or sled, impossible to trace
from these frail maps, the wind howling across
the twisting canyons in the sea,
the moulins running with ice water
pattern of their own design.

King Tide
Toby Fitch

we don't always take stock of
or shed our satellite stocks but a blonde woman
pointing at maps became historical and the moon shone
hysterically on our sector
                                we embraced our shelves
for a large complex weather event
an east coast low that we panicked very carefully about
below a fat tsunami cloud
its every wish and wash like policy breaking the air
waves we saw at least a hundred and fifty
cubic metres of sand gone
                                  lying and gushing about the street
people asked the sea why it had geared up negatively
the prime minister praised the storm for creating
new lucrative-warm waterfront estates
further inland on scenic new river systems
                                          he was spilling over
bubbling on camera gas eeked from his seams
it was like he'd been mined by his own
sense of the public gaze
                royally
weighing in on the storm which seemed also
for most of its duration to be at war with various other wars
mostly digital and cultural ones that the media
or at least the media we didn't have active stakes in
blew up and out of proportion with
the kind of inflammatory commentary
straight out of the textbook on bushfires and cyclones
it was hell
          mental at the end of the dayglo
hi-vis and off in the west with a few helicopters
dewing the rounds
                     but a certain kind of peace
the moving forward kind had to be made
so the land was employed to right the ship

and the flora and fauna engaged
in the labour that would solidify the electorate
who'd become shaky on all the conflicting beetle grounds
that needed to be shored up
                           because time doesn't
mean anything when you're about to have Walter lapping
at your door he was phenomenal
contractually speaking his rivers' tributes to Ares
included roots and trunks of many
wrong-time-wrong-place trees
and snake effigies hollowed out and named
after other hallowed dignitaries of the prefab past
participle government
                         although no matter what
Walter employed to stem the time
signatures kept mounting up for a cap to unsuit
the foreign suits who were lining up
which was mean
                  we all thought
an anti-everything mentality had come home to roast
or was it a spit
                i can't be onshore
all i know is that it was spinning and revolutions
only last so long or shift their shop
into other regions of the globe like hot or cold y-fronts
so we were all good our behaviour
once the clean-up job had blown over heads
wasn't in question
                      we could go on going about our busyness
of acquiring new states of mind to rent out
to embody with avatars or to have digested by
our huge accumulation of mouth pieces
                                    we'd amassed
all the personal profiles of those who'd floundered
and the platforms we'd virtually divested of them were all
ready in the crosswinds anyway
                    and anyhow
havens were being founded on cities of foam
                                   we built on

and on the cultural wastelands and the driftwood
things were floating around at such opportune angles
and to such a positive degree in the tide
it was only natural that we adapt the landscape
had shifted it was a truly wonderful time
to be   offshore
       invested in our futures

Operations
Andy Jackson

GP referral to specialist (24.5.1976)

    this 5 year old boy

        I have been able to re-assure his
mother about the former, but the latter is
worrying her, particularly as the father
as a result of severe

    could you please   outline his
future

letter from professor of paediatrics (17.9.1982)

    we like to
        feel quite certain
            abnormality
        the very characteristic
            opinion

        disorder of the connective
  I think
suspect
        mild or even serious
          really serious problems

            a little
bit of nuisance
    this process should be repeated
        allowed to progress to a severe stage
            to give   a very simple

and factual description
    just a name
        just what he feels
          an error
    cropping up

operation sheet (7.1.1987)

complicating through the old
incision down into
      the possible
to expose the sacral
         the fusion mass
wires sublaminar wires double wires
contoured rods into the wings
      of the ilium
         moderate correction but remarkable
            how rigid the spine
stripped and decorticated and bone
      graft laid out on the concave
wounds were all
      closed this lad
         has lost
            a lot of blood
1590 mls he can be
mobilised when into a low
sort of brace satis
factory

nurse's progress sheet (8-15.1.1987)

tolerating	quiet	drain continues
as ordered	tolerating this	reasonably
unsettled	gauze	found at 8am
leaking	dressing	reinforced
some relief	light diet	not very
interested	bile stained	fluid no visitors
pressure care	morphine	a small bleed
quite settled	co-operative	from mid-back
sitting	on edge	unsupported
tends to lose	balance	looks pale still
slight	down	unsettled early in the

evening found half out of bed at 11.25pm with his feet on the floor
awaiting signature   dis or iented   needs

encouragement   quiet and in   tact
obs stable   hair washed   brace re al
igned   and he stood up and walked

a few steps for discharge tomorrow home

letter from mother (23.1.1987)

dear
    we hardly know
               but
the   extra
        regular
trauma of a hospital stay
            the whole person
    in isolation
                wonderful
      operation
anxiety of the days
      we couldn't have chosen

see you when we come back

The breadth of the moment

Kristen Lang

The bald woman is in the distance. Her clothes
cover all of her body – the coat is heavy, the flat-heeled
boots give a broadness to the sway of her gait. She steps
through as many cities, as many towns and homes
as there are ways to live in them, and is seen only in glimpses.
She wears too the keffiyeh, the high-heels, the hand-me-downs,
the socks with no shoes, the gnarled hands, the slipped-disc spine,
the glamour, the joy and the tiredness, the conviction,
the blindness, though she is never blind.

She is both roads where the way divides. She is the tremor
in each moment of tenderness. We sense her near to us –
she becomes the breath mark between this word and another,
like a chance. She is the weight of all heartbeats – ant to crocodile,
raven to whale. She is the closeness of this bug, this
fern, that human. She is all of us, she is stone. And neither right
nor wrong, neither this creed nor another, she is the enemy
of the state, of the self, of the holy books, and of every law.
She is the mesh and the swarm of us, she is each

one of us, she is the waste dump and the polluted swell
of the sea, she is the robot and the space probe and the music
the army plays as it powers down after a raid.
The woman lifts onto her shoulders the singer, the scientist,
the teacher, the child, and each thinks they remember her.
She carries the rent left behind in the wake of every tree,
and the shouts of the folk who are fighting, and the cries
of each victory. She is all of us. Every choice. Every breeze.
Every call. Every seed. And she is silent.

The breadth of her. If we knew it, pressing into us,
we'd be her ourselves. All of her. Without divide. The woman
raises her face, her blue-green eyes in the star-punctured frame
of our being here. We would speak to her. Our voice
a rejoining. What to say? How much can we explain?
She carries us. And glimpsing her, for a moment, in the corners
of our eyes, we hold hands – on trains, in backyards, across
walls, across oceans. She opens her mouth – we hear
the orbit of the Earth. And we say? Night falls –

our shadows become Earth's shadow. Or day arrives –
the Earth's shadow, our shadows. And we say: forgive us. And:
so many selves. She is born of time, slipping forward
around all of us. The hour spins. We choose how it
falls from us. The woman curves under Mars, over Venus,
black holes and new-born stars behind her. We turn to each other, still
holding hands – today, today we are this hill, this blue-gum,
this fur seal, we are the albatross and the huon pine. And look.
The moment arriving. And again. Her heat where we touch.

For the woman, every wall is a lie. The day-night
enfolding us. How nothing is ours. And we say? We say:
this air we breathe, this dawn, this bird calling, this rain – our arms,
raised. Our hearts: our witness.

Box Brownie Album

John Watson

1. Here is Harry
   on his boat moored at Port Hacking
   which Mary once said described his cough.
   On the beach Glenda, half
   jokingly says it wasn't the cough
   that carried him off
   but the coffin they carried him off in.

2. A boffin reading Nathaniel West
   on a deckchair on deck;
   here's baby Celeste
   who will in a few years tickle
   the ivories and play
   Fur Elise for her friend Elise,
   then find herself with Harry up
   the Georges River without a paddle.

3. In the saddle Roslyn
   appears nonchalant, soon to Begin
   the Beguine even when
   on horseback looking into the sun.

4. Charlene is almost naked but somehow
   supremely chaste on the banana chair
   with an overexposed air

   like someone standing in the prow
   of a becalmed dhow
   with a surprised poodle.

5. Oodles of washed out grey-green,
   a swimming pool about as vague
   as only chlorinated water can be,

the surface like the transparent raincoat
which has slipped from the shoulders
of the person standing beside it (the pool)
looking towards a distant galaxy.

6.. Lax raffia lampshade,
a Fler chair,
a laminated coffee table,
the plastic deep-buttoned bar front,
the ribbed glass door
open on to the landscape.
The camera letting in the light.

7. A bright harbour view:
water like a pegged-out
ruffled plastic ground sheet,
one tree just making it into view,
the opposite land mass so far off
it offers thin portions
of sliced nougat.

8. Agar-agar cake on a Lazy Susan,
A-line dresses showing brave knees,
cigarettes at half-mast.

9. O.S. and well-dressed under the Eiffel Tower,
most of it invisible,
Harry and the boys
almost in Maupassant's favoured location (on it
where it can't be seen.)
Harry's chintz wife, Frieda.

10. Ted, Ned and Fred,
three would-be Astaires in *Top Hat*
posing carefully and not
mussing up their white ties.

11. Tied up on slips, a sloop;
Sea front; an abandoned
fuel depot, oyster leases so far off
as to look like a fine-toothed comb.

12. Norma in a brunch coat a beautiful
    shade of apricot shown to advantage
    on the red brick balcony,
    smoking and drinking beer.
    Also on view: Styrofoam, a discarded
    washing-up rack, what might be a telescope.

13. Hoping to be at their best
    George, Lynton, Armand, Garcia, George ("Cat")
    during a bit of a spat
    with sibling rivalry and then some
    over the meaning of "indenture", George
    with rising gorge insisting it means
    something to do with "toothpaste."

14. Narrow-waisted Nora in the hippiastrum glasshouse,
    the flowers open to show their gums
    like horses wide-open-mouthed
    or hippopotamuses taking a bath.

15. Beth with yawning hippiastrums (a close-up)
    still (the flowers) like a horse showing its teeth
    but also like wax funerary blooms
    or a velvet Trocadero corsage.

16. On the Corso
    a man, a plan, Panama.
    The cryptic on Saturday on the patio.

17. A paling fence, a ladder, tidal baths.
    Posing in their striped swimmers
    Alec, Henry and Adrian,
    and between Henry and Alec,
    Betty Crawford or Joan Gable.

18. A table under an oilcloth,
    Shipping lanes ditto;
    an island light-nano-seconds away;
    underlit shoreline made to look like
    opened halves of a Vegemite sandwich.

19. And which twin is it in the small galley
    of the narrow ferry? Alec or George?
    Always difficult to tell apart
    in uniform. Somewhere in this lacqueria
    is the sombre sentiment (casting anchor
    in the Georges River of time)
    of Lamartine's *Le Lac*.

20. Ric pictured outside,
    beside the ashlar bonfire site
    against the fibro outhouse,
    reading the Kama Sutra,
    is no calmer, is flaunting karma,
    shouting at the camera.

21. In what may be Cammeray,
    what appears to be a folly
    and beside it what might be Harry
    and, standing in a vestibule,
    what can only be Sally
    in a wedding dress in white guipure
    draped in what seems like holly
    uncertain whether to marry.

22. Harry again almost mother-of-pearl;
    George scanning for a whale,
    Merle lolling at the tiller
    as if their runabout were a plough
    and the sky and sea too long fallow.

23. Hollowed by dredging it would seem,
    the old Kodak makes the lake
    look entirely uneventful.
    Equally uneventful, Reg, Les and Raoul
    apparently frozen while drinking tea.

24. Lee bringing out scones;
    lumber and what would seem lumps of amber
    amidst a general air of slumber
    in a yard with a single oleander

        suggesting in the shadows – under
        the car hoist in an oil slick
        of black and white and black –
        a half-hidden Panda.

25.   And a pale blue Skoda
        in the back seat of which
        Glen and Lyn managed a coda
        based on *Lady Chatterley's Lover*
        which had been smuggled in
        by someone on the Orsova from Suva.

26.   Over where boats are zigzagging
        in and out through river algae
        and the water itself conveys ennui,

        the place has the vacuity of a yard
        from which Captain and Mary Marvel
        have zoomed into a Shazam cloud.

27.   The yard also seems odd,
        as if an ice carver lived here
        and an ice-carved Medusa
        had melted a week earlier,
        or sky-divers had once landed beside the Hills Hoist.

28.   *Proofs*
        Just an overview which may go some way
        towards explaining what might otherwise seem
        a merely random tour of blast-furnace, bay,

        waste shore, trampoline, various
        chook sheds, car-ports, grass huts,
        Notre Dame (in gay Paree before gay

        was to be lost to the language), red
        tulips, tents, Carol looking like Ali McGraw
        in *Love Story*, Glenda raking up seaweed,

and all the reunions of The Night, the Shed,
of the Rhyming Couples – Ron and Yvonne
Harry and Carrie, Ned and Fred,

Francis and Frances. This buffalo grass back
yard, with single mulberry and amputee frangipani,
a yard just big enough to house Siliac

was Harry's grandmother's. The glimpse of shore,
of water and the back fence
was Carrs Park, now a carpark. The war

was over. Harry met Mary at the Hurstville Odeon,
in the rodeo past, fixed in egg albumen
and albumised in black and white. Then

the camping trips, the Port Hacking shack,
the Fred Astaire look-alike contest, various
fibro sheds, the trips to Fiji and back,

the trick handshakes, the walls of tyres.
Harry and Mary were married at Wanda Beach
but Glenda had a thing for Harry

and disappeared for years. The Bay of Islands high tide,
the Glaciarium, the hippeastrum colony,
Paris and Port Kembla, all followed,

and an out-of-focus Kerry when he or she
followed Glenda to Suva. Rose
pictured with roses, an emu farm, a plush

party for Carol's divorce, Sally's crush
on someone at Mooney Mooney,
all captured by Celeste's Box Brownie.

The Mill Road
Kevin Smith

He woke in the charcoal dark and put
his work clothes on in the narrow passage
between the iron bed and the wardrobe's
brown veneer. She stirred and sat up
and wiped sleep from her eyes, and the window,
where she looked, was a black vault
open on eternity. She reached for her dressing
gown and felt the coming dawn.

The boy held his bedroom door
ajar. The father walked past
and flicked the switch. A dull yellow
filled the gloom, and the boy drew back
into his room.
                        In the laundry,
the father splashed freezing water
on his face. The pipes groaned
like a loaded winch. He took a towel
from the nail beside the window opaque
with frost. The blank face of some
bespoke future.
                        She packed the firebox
tight with iron bark and opened the flue,
took a cast iron pan from a hook
above the stove. As she dropped
tea into a pot, he rolled
a smoke and checked for snow.
                        At
the stove he put his arms around her.
She nudged him off to chop an onion
and fry an egg. She put the porridge
on for the clutch of kids who filled
bare rooms with sleeping breath.

                              At the back
door he pulled his work boots on.
They looked at one another. He stepped
outside and cold air bullied
its way in; she woke the kids
for school.
            They crowded the stove. 'Where's
your brother?' At the bedroom window
he watched his father footslog the mill
road, a dank shadow cuffed
to a reprobate sky. He snuck out
the back door. The mother at the dishes.
'Where are you goin'?' The door banged shut.

His father's boots left prints in icy
sludge. He jumped from print to print
and landed short each time but kept
on trying. The hooter sounded at
the mill. The father turned and saw
the boy at his game. 'Go on home
for Christ's sake!' Some mute thing
stood between them. 'I said get home!'

A log truck buckling under its load
crawled the bend out of a cloud-
drowned world. Brute metal
and beheld momentum shouldered cold
air off the road. Its roar mauled
the quiet. The boy leapt aside.
The truck pushed on toward the mill.
A rag nailed to a log flapped
at the back of the truck: a shredded hand,
or the sacrament of a forsaken god.
The boy looked back to the house, then back
to the mill.
            It had no walls; machinery
shivered in the wind. The twin blades

of the Canadian—tall as a man—stood
in silhouette against a reluctant
dawn. Blitzes idled in the cold
air, doorless, without windscreens,
waiting for the day to begin. Men
—cryptic in the mist—trudged
the yard and warmed their hands at fire
drums. The boy lobbed a knot
of wood into a bank of smouldering
bark—opened it up like a saw
cut. Vermilion coals flared
in a colourless landscape. The father turned.
Beyond, smoke dribbled from chimneys,
the houses a sniffling cluster of chilblained
boxes. 'Go on the hell home for
the last time,' he said, and followed
the men into the mill.
                                              The overseer
stood fast—arms folded and face
hard against the cold—and waited
for the boy to go.
                       The Blitzes skidded
in the muddy yard. The Canadian whined
to life, searching blindly to find
the momentum to flitch the first log
of the morning. Above the mill smoke
bloomed white.
                    The day got colder, and the boy
turned for home. On the mill road
his father's footprints—the few that remained—
went one way, the boy's another.

And the sky dropped its basket of snow.

Desert flaneurs
K A Nelson

1. The bureaucrat

No suit, no tie, no top hat on his head
no polished leather shoes, no brass-
handled cane—the desert flaneur
comes dressed for comfort:
short sleeved cotton shirt,
loose cotton slacks,
Akubra for a bit of shade.

He moves around the settlement
clipboard in one hand, Mont Blanc
pen in the other, ticking off a list
in crimson ink. There's perspiration
on his upper lip, his underarms,
perhaps his crotch . . .
He curses the temperature
and his bloody awful job.

The flies, the stench, the upturned
rubbish bins (three ticks),
the feral donkey problem (tick),
the dogs, all interbred,
look full of ticks to him.
He gives that box two ticks
for emphasis.

His latest model four-wheel drive
awaits, like Charon's skiff, to sail
him out of Hades, back across
the Styx. The river's dry
and sandy here,
beyond the cattle grid.

This afternoon he'll take
his clipboard back to town,
review his list,
shower, sink a few
long necks (Full Strength),
compose a succinct
analysis for the Government,
hammer home his message.

2. The Local Government Inspector

I fly in on the mailplane—a not unpleasant flight—
no other passengers detract, no unnecessary queries,
no bugger chundering in bags . . . The Council Clerk
is there to pick me up, take me to lunch. At the compound,
a German Shepherd the Council Clerk calls *Goebbels*,
is forcibly restrained. A six-foot chain link fence is,
he claims, a necessity. It keeps the local vermin out.
He likes to garden. I suspect the sprinkling system came
from the Works Department, but who am I to judge?
Lunch is salad, freshly picked, cold leftover lamb.
A pinot noir is offered and declined—this settlement
is 'dry'. We settle for a glass of aqua minerale,
a dash of lime. The inspection takes two hours.
I observe Essential Services still runs well.
The Council Clerk has a Good Man in charge, but
the dickhead likes to stir the Good Man up, in front
of me. That's one black mark. The Workyard's
been vandalised, again. The Council Clerk says, *I know
who dunnit—three little shits with nothin' better to do
but trifle with me 'ead.* I wonder if he's on medication?
The garbage tip's the Clerk's pride and joy, fenced
and locked each afternoon at 5pm. He's had fun
with an excavator, dug two great bloody holes he's
proud of—one for general household rubbish, one for
animals found dead—I counted a dozen donkey carcasses
when I peered in. When asked why so many, the Clerk
replied, *The silly fuckers got 'emselves locked in an empty
house—you shudda smelt the smell, seen the flies. What a
shitfest. I got my 2.I.C to clean it up, then he quit,
the squeamish git.* There's a pile of metal—old car bodies,
fridges, angle iron, another labelled 'plastic' and one
for worn out tyres. All very neat, this garbage tip—
his one big tick. Pity about the settlement—it looks sick.
The Council office runs like clockwork. Angela keeps a lid
on things, wears the trousers. I'm is pretty sure the Council
Clerk slips her a bit of 'you know what' after working hours.
All in all he's doing fine. Not ten out of ten but maybe nine.
The local staff are satisfied, as far as I can tell. The trouble-
maker I heard from last time has relocated to the clinic

where she plays merry hell with pharmaceuticals. So *he*
tells me. Back at the airfield, I make small talk with the pilot,
who seems so young, he should be back in high school,
or britches, but he's no fool. He's getting flying hours up
to move on from mail planes to ten seaters in the Top End,
come the dry. HQ should be happy with my report. I predict
the Clerk will stay on quite a while. My take on him? Ninety-
nine per cent 'mercenary', not a scrap of 'missionary', a little
bit of 'misfit' thrown in.

3. The Minister and his First Assistant Secretary

the minister for Aborigines may
drop into your community
if convenient, if it's not too far off
a highway or it's near a town or city

he'll exchange pleasantries
with local dignitaries
over lunch that you provide . . .
that'll keep him on side

>	chartered plane
>	tight timeframe
>	fly in fly out
>	one trough, one snout

the minister may bring his right hand man
a first assistant secretary
who only likes to fly first class
he's top dog at last
don't dare call him a horse's arse
or he'll make your lives a misery
with his white supremacist policies
and he'll still be there long after
the Minister or his ministry

Grief Wears a Body
Mark Tredinnick

GRIEF WEARS a body,
                and today she stands in mine.
The rose bush by my stoop, flush with blooms that flared
In seven long unearthly days of heat,
                bends at daybreak toward the east,
Beneath a night of heavy rain. Nothing readies you
For when it wants to leave. You learn to grieve
                by grieving, and nothing must rush the work.

Rain will fell you earthward;
                be in no haste to rise. Grief lasts as long
As love was deep. Mourning is work that chooses you
Exactly when you want it least.
                I want to say it's work that doesn't pay,
But there's a living you earn by putting in the time.
Grief pays for what it takes by all it gives.
                Is grieving the living

The hardest grief to learn,
                the most like death, itself?
You know my story now: three children I used to live with live
With me now in pictures
                I've posted on my wall. And how I miss
Them only my body knows: my left hip is where
My daughter lives, and how it aches at dawn.
                I bend, like the rose

In prayer that weighs me down,
                             and there she is in how I let her go.
My elder boy inhabits my right arm,
A bicep I work too hard at weights I lift
To give back to my body the waiting work
                          my mind's too fast do. And where
Is my middle boy? That lion lives in by toes,
                            numb with age and boots I wore

That never really fit.
               This is the alchemy of sorrow, that *rust*
Upon the soul: to teach you how to dwell in what you've lost, and it
To dwell in you, making absence over into presence more profound.
Grief is a body that only knows how
                    to heal by how it hurts. Until it doesn't so much
Anymore. I tie the rose. My children prick
                    my finger there and laugh,
                          and all the weather clears.

NOTE
that rust/ upon the soul: I have in mind "*Ever'thing there is but lovin' leaves a rust on yo' soul*," from Langston Hughes's *Not Without Laughter*.

Driver
Vidhya Karnamadakala

From port to Centre, the driver
transports them one by one,
beads on a broken abacus.
The rear-view mirror shows
bodies in auto-pilot;
shoulders hunched into fuel-reserve,
an odometer of tender blisters
recording the miles fled in blood-soaked dust,
torn airbags in chests grasping
shallow breath from sickness for a home
that exiled them.
Terror and uncertainty ebbs
like hot liquid into the troughs
and glades of their minds,
purloining the memories that give identity,
leaving behind only practiced movements.
Speak. Silence. Papers.
Scatter. Gather. Wait.

At dusk as the sky wills itself blind,
the driver eats dinner with his wife.
They lap a familiar route of conversation,
an odometer of sighs recording the miles
lost to an expired frequent flyer card,
fog-light eyes squinting at newspaper
and paperback, parked on
either side of the coffee table.
Cruise control takes the garbage out,
wipes the kitchen top. Television.
Tea (lemon myrtle). Sleep.

The driver and his passengers move
in auto-pilot;
One designed by insouciance,
the other dictated by survival.
One circled by Cooktown orchids,
the other by razor mesh fence

and chants to
go back
illegal migrants.

Sometimes he kept sweets
for the children,
handing it to them at the boom gate,
dazzled by how their eyes glittered—
like starlight traversing
from distant globes that were already long gone.
He just didn't know it yet.

Equations for a Falling Body
Sarah Holland-Batt

The railing on the balcony in question
        is iron spiked with fleurs-de-lis—
hip-height, hits right at the pivot point
        where a tipple at a right angle
would hurtle you fifteen storeys
        smack into concrete & bursting
like a taut sack of honey—especially
        if you're tottering in heels (she was) & bent
on ending it (his story). The apartment: faux art deco,
        fourteen hundred a week. An ironic fresco
in the lobby, all putti & blousy clouds
        in fairy floss green & pink. A swatch of harbour
below the bedroom window—impasto of swell,
        water navy as Whiteley's midnight studio
or a luminol-washed crime scene. She's done
        the place in soft furnishings—mohair throws,
peachy sheepskin—everything furred like the pelts
        in the South African ecolodge where they spooned
on honeymoon—height of the headover-
        heels phase, rolling on the four-poster,
mosquito netting floating over her body
        like a bloodstained veil. He trains seven days
a week, hundreds of reps in a skin-tight tee,
        jacked to Jesus with roids & supplements.
Jugular hard as a metal stent in his neck,
        brawler's shoulders, slab of meat saddled
with pecs. He postures like a great ape, all strut
        & front, rubs his thighs with Vasoline
to stop the chafe. Bruiser by night & trader
        by day. Suits: cliché Armani in predator shades—
charcoal, ash, nurse shark grey. She used
        to dance ballet. Since she quit, her muscles
atrophied—a diet of cocaine & laxatives
        will do this—& standing en pointe is a torture
worse than her Laboutins with their seven inch
        hike. He never liked her dancing anyway—
just an excuse to flirt & sashay, & how could he

be sure she was at the studio?
She left dolled up like a whore—fuchsia
    sports bra & mesh cutout leggings—
an open invitation for other men. He let loose,
    laid down the law. Now she's sulky, bored.
She misses salsa? He doesn't give a shit,
    she's testing his patience with this
I miss the girls refrain. The hell she did.
    Give her an inch & she'll sneak out
god knows where—trout pout porny
    & painted ice pink, scouse brow two shades
darker than her hair: fried strawberry, overdone
    with GHDs. He can't trust her as far
as he can throw… No, that's not how it is—
    he just loves her so much
he gets jealous. It's only natural.
    Besides, pixel by pixel she's beautiful
& he should know, he's got pinhole
    lenses studding the ceiling, a live dashcam feed
from her Audi, spyware trawling her emails
    for evidence of infidelity or insolence,
surveys & supervises her like a grounded teen.
    Your calls may be monitored is a joke he likes
to make after inspecting her texts.
    She laughs less these days. Fifty contacts
in her phone but only three dialled
    the last six weeks: mother, sister, shrink.
The ringtone is Beyoncé, Single Ladies
    & of course the irony's her knuckleduster—
cabochon the size of the Ritz, peppered with emeralds.
    He locked that down. No joke. He likes to choke
her with a belt during sex—*Consensual,* he says,
    when detectives find it stashed under the bed;
I'm not a psycho. Dental records show effects of purging—
    damage to the enamel. Smashed to smithereens
in the end, unrecognisable: that much we know.
    Over the last month, a low pressure front
building before a Southerly buster—his temper,
    impossible demands: her ass needs work,
does she own any clothes less stripperesque, get some *class,*
    & why is she eye-fucking the waiter?

He's not an idiot. He's going to kill her
      if she keeps playing games. She lays low,
makes plans. Tells her sister in London to expect her,
      warns her mother to call the cops
if she goes incommunicado. Hops on standby
      at her psychologist's. Finds him waiting
in the parking lot after yoga—*just checking*
      in, he says, & grins like the sadist
he is. *I'm frightened* is what she writes
      in her oddly childish diary—pattern
of purple iris on the cover, gold padlock—
      I can't live like this. She comes home
to roses—forty-eight, extra long-stemmed
      in an ominous white box laid on the bed
like a child's coffin. *Sorry I get so possessive,*
      the note says. *You do my head in.* The flights
are booked for Thursday, Heathrow, longhaul
      & so what's the harm in one last dinner—
a final balancing act on the high-wire—
      so she pours herself into his favourite bodycon
dress—ribbed straps across her breasts,
      a mummy's wrappings, de rigeur red.
He meets her on the curb in his chartreuse Lotus,
      doors flicked upwards like a cricket's legs,
zooms them both to Rockpool for yellowfin
      carpaccio, trio of sourdough & spreads,
dry-aged eye fillet, carafe of Côtes du Rhône,
      then a lemon meringue nest they share.
Vodka on the rocks post-dinner, then another—
      his raised voice cutting through the clatter.
She said she was scared, that much
      a witness at the next table remembers.
At the time it was crazy to think
      it meant anything, she testifies, *more than*
a charged conversation. If only we'd known.
      For the record, the jury is shown CCTV—
the Lotus pulling into his parking space erratically,
      her head a pale moon in the windscreen.
He's talking, slams the steering wheel.
      A beat. They sit side by side, buckled
in their seats. The doors rise. They exit.

What happens next is unseen—an argument
out of frame, although the camera in the lift
    catches him dragged her in by the neck.
They ascend. The rest beyond description—less
    than a minute & she's tumbling through air—
seventeen stories of steel & glass
    rocketing past at highway speed,
her Louis Vuitton still slung over her shoulder—
    then it's over: sick thud on pavement,
chaos where her body should have been.
    He couldn't hold her back if he tried
is what his lawyer says at trial. *She had a death wish.*
    Tonight was the night. The equations
for a falling body are complex—experts
    attest she wasn't close to terminal
velocity, though well above the waterline
    emergency doctors call seven storeys to heaven—
altitude at which a fall is fatal. Fifteen
    storeys equals utter annihilation: impact
like a gunnysack dropped onto concrete. Best
    guess she met her maker at over
a hundred & twenty ks, four long seconds
    for the entire fall. Footage is shown
of the seconds after—his controlled descent
    to street level in the elevator
clutching his head, then raising
    both arms like he's under arrest—
the sheer unfiltered panic of a man
    who's forgotten he's live on air.
At trial he tenders her mental state
    as evidence—Stillnox, anti-anxiety meds,
a cocktail to deaden stress. *Her choice,* he says,
    shaking his head, dejected—parody
of grieving spouse. She was barely allowed to leave
    the house, the prosecutor scoffs
on cross—trots out her diary with its litany
    of intimidations. He can't explain the note
found in her jeans—*there are cameras*
    inside the house & out, scrawled in hasty cursive,
intended for god knows who, some friend
    who tried to help. She had an acute fear

of heights—why suicide by jumping? It took him
        by surprise, he says. *I held her wrists,*
but she slipped out of my grasp. The defence rests.
        He takes a shaky sip of water. Nobody's convinced
except his new girlfriend, who sobs & nurses
        her tissue box as he's led out of the dock.
The sentence when it comes is no shock—
        thirty years in an airless cell, twenty
with good behaviour. *He wanted to be her saviour—*
        we'll never know what was in her head,
his lawyer says in the presser. The tanned anchor
        at midday reports he's facing thirty years.
Facing. Of course he'll appeal. A short reel
        of a cop pushing his head into a van, then the news
moves on. Afternoon—a huge gale that grounds
        the planes, howls through the headlands.
Glaring light over the harbour—whitecaps & mica-flecks
        of sun breaking in a ferry's wake.
Norfolk pines bend & whistle in the park
        as sailboats tack & nudge forward—
each pushing its skinful of air
        in a single unbroken arc.

The Wee-Vee
B.R. Dionysius

For Clifford Olds, 20; Ronald "Tubby" Endicott, 18; and Louis "Buddy" Costin, 21.

(i)

No one performs a c-section on the *Wee-Vee* as they do
on the capsized *Oklahoma*, its hull motionless as a whale's
carcass. The operation is tricky. Air rushes out of the tiny
spyholes boilermakers cut into the metal plates to locate
trapped men & air pockets dissolve. Some heave lunches
as sailors drown looking up into the small cones of light
that penetrate through the bullet-hole sized punctures in
the ship's hull. Divers keep an eye on blowouts that will
disembowel, oil & gasoline in the water; their intestines
coiling like rope as welding sparks ignite trapped gasses.
Salvage crews become expert at ripping up steel sections
as if they are rotten floorboards. Through these keyholes,
hardened dockers turn their faces away as able seamen scull
seawater to get it over with; following the grizzled veterans'
advice on how to die quickly as their last order of the day.

(ii)

West Virginia upright, sinks to the muddy floor of Pearl Harbor;
a behemoth hooked catfish that wrestles into the river's bottom
& will not budge. Counter-flooding orders kills Olds, Endicott
& Costin sixteen days later, but save many others on the stricken
battleship, averting capsize. Bulkheads are sealed as men struggle
through rising seawater; trudging mud-shod in a swamp.
Heavy iron doors clang into place, church bells knelling the ones
who didn't make it past the closed hatches to their doom. Life is
a long military drill that ends with accidental death & a taut telegram
home. The vessel bleeds internally from six torpedo stab wounds,
the vast weight of the oily sea pushes its victim under the port's
briny water, drowning the warship in this surprise mafioso hit.

(iii)

The *Wee-Vee* burns for thirty hours. Fire-crews liken it to
trying to put out hell. Beside the smoldering ruins of four
battleships, jumpy guards are posted along the docks
& scan the horizon for another attack or even invasion.
They watch the black sails of oil-slicks clot like fried grease
in a pan. For days, coastguard crews pull the flotsam &
jetsam of burnt bodies from the harbor with fishing gaffs
& poles. At first they think the banging is wreckage slapping
with the tide's pull, but the regular tapping beats out a morse
code of human tragedy. There are men alive forty feet below.
A tattoo of wrenches plays its big bass sound, but the marines
cannot stand its melody. Some injure themselves to leave
the sad concert early or go AWOL to escape the drumming
dirge the ship utters. All know, there is no way to rescue
its ghostly, marooned crew.

(iv)

Deep below in the ship's bow, three sailors are entombed
in a dark pumping station; Clifford Olds, Ronald Endicott
& Louis Costin, the eldest merely twenty-one. Their drill
practice saved them from drowning, leaving their air-tight
compartment dry. They know that on the other side of the
hatch, death uses seawater to gargle their friends. Barn-warm,
they wonder what the hell happened. 'Buddy' Costin grabs
a flashlight & swears it was a sixteen inch shell that accidentally
exploded, maybe a few. That maybe the magazine went up.
'Tubby' Endicott, thin & tall, with ten months experience
up his sleeve shakes his head, thinks it more likely torpedoes
as the explosions all raked portside & besides he tells them,
if it was the mag they wouldn't be here, but blasted to hell.
Cliff pipes up & whispers that if topside can hear them they
will be saved. Divers will come for them bringing air tanks
& welding gear. Maybe even some kind of experimental
Navy diving bell to rescue them.

(v)

So they take shifts with chisels & hammers, arms jarring
at the impact of steel on iron. They are the ship's faint pulse,
sending a simple message throughout its vast complicated
system, their will to live travels as sound waves along the
salty relays of their vessel's bloodstream. The vibrations,
electrical signals that energise the *Wee-Vee's* breached hull,
then escape forty feet up through the harbor's cauldron &
into the guards' ears above. Their homecoming is not over
'Buddy' argues so long as the top brass know they exist,
down in the rabbit hole in which they have fallen. After all
the navy has a duty to their men. So they bang their drums
slowly until callouses thicken on their palms & hands ache
as though crushed in a favourite wrestler's grip. The pump
room has emergency rations, fresh water, flashlights, batteries,
but no means of escape. 'Tubby' makes it his job to mark
the calendar off every morning with a red cross like a child
counting down days to his birthday. An eight-day clock
gives them no extra time in their black prison, but their
Xs will mark the spot right up until Christmas Eve.

(vi)

Cliff rations the ration cartons. They lap up fresh water
from their battle station. On the tenth day the batteries
begin to run out so 'Tubby' orders one torch to be saved
for marking the calendar only. Costin scratches curses
into the bulkhead, his last words like a convicted man
going to the gallows. Words his mother will never hear
him say. Out loud in the stale air 'Tubby' prays that there
will enough juice left in America to rise up & defeat the
ferrymen who has rowed them all toward god so soon,
in this their first battle. Costin tells him to save his breath.
They all agree to go down swinging together. None will
commit the mortal sin. On the fifteenth day the darkness
descends into their bodies & wraps their lungs in its tight
black silk. The have eaten up all the air. Holding each other's
hands, 'Tubby' leads them with the last of the torch light
into the storeroom & tucks his friends into bed on a shelf.

He makes sure that their uniforms are straight, shirts
tucked in. That they are presentable for death's inspection.
They try to have one last smoke, but their cigarettes won't light.

(vii)

In the last breaths of their dreams they see the *Wee-Vee* raised
from the dead; a soaking lazarus given one more chance to live.
They feel the heat from the welding that patches new iron skin
over her old wounds, smell the fresh paint that combats metal's
ageless adversary - rust. They stand at ease on the *Wee-Vee's*
new deck watching marines raise a flag on Mount Suribachi.
They recoil in their hammocks from her sixteen inch guns
that flatten Iwo Jima, Okinawa; pulverize roads, men, vehicles,
ammo-stores, pill-boxes, turning all into black volcanic sand.
They see the landing craft heading shoreward like hundreds of tadpoles,
chains of frogspawn swimming toward the beaches, wobbly legs
breaching waves, tight lungs filling up with air for the last time.
This amphibious invasion wrecking the island's stubborn habitat.
They fire the ship's ack ack guns to celebrate the atomic surrender.
Finally, they steam into Tokyo Bay, now that war is over.

(viii)

The hatch to pump room A-109 squeals like a piggery.
The salvage crew expect to find the same scene as they
have found in all of her flooded compartments, men
reduced to simple cells; a tepid precambrian sea & stale
gases devoid of any life, a briny soup, a polluted harbor
berth when a ship dumps its ballast. They are surprised
then when they enter the dry hold like Carter breaking
into Tutankhamen's tomb & make their gasp of discovery.
Three uniformed bodies lying together; hands on chests
as if sleeping. Some are reminded of Scott's antarctic end,
the explorers lying frozen in a last salute of comradeship,
then oblivion. The salvage workers take in the end of
this tragic play when all is still & silent as the curtain falls.
They weep at the messages left behind, the calendar crossed
out neatly up to December the twenty-third. In Costin's

locker a lady's wristwatch is found, a christmas gift for
his mother he never sent. She has it repaired & wears
her son's gift for the next forty years, each tiny tick
of the minute hand is her lost son chiming in her ear.
Others remember dancing, mad waltzes around the kitchen,
giving the teachers a hard time& the smell of leather
as the credits rolled on *The Great Dictator.*

(ix)

At the *Monkey Bar* Jack Miller rounds on the original
waitress who expects some sleazy pick-up line, but she
receives a double-exposed face; one glad that she still
has the negative of that photo; the other her own sad
hustle, weighed down by the snapshots of possibly
hundreds of dead sailors wound tight in her purse.
There is no charge for the negative, she has saved them
as thin celluloid men, their last organic manifestation.
Stolen a dimension from Cliff Olds rendering the boy
in only two planes. In the photograph they sit on wicker
chairs, Clifford looks at the camera, looks through
the waitress. He dies not know it yet, but this is where
his gaze stops. His glass doesn't quite reach his friends
in time, as they clink their shots together, a noise
like anchor chains scraping the *Wee-Vee's* bow rolls
around their table. Bourbon swills in their stomachs.
A packet of *Camels* lies on the table, a lit one in his
left hand; they all smoke. Jack & Frank (another friend
who dies three years later) do not look at the camera,
but to where their drinks strike their iceberg warning
note. None of them buy the photo, what a scam they
joke as the tired waitress moves on to another table
of boys from the *Tennessee.* Like the sailors, her family
is poor & any surplus money is sent home so her
parents can buy bonds; funding the great war
for America's civilisation.

Wherever this is it's where we are
Alison Flett

after Terrance Hayes

the southern tip of a southern land where all that matters is tonight
at the Wheaty & thedarkthatsurroundsus & words. We're strung-out
under fairy lights, high on Sonic Prayer IPA, waiting for what's to come.
L is waving to someone at the bar but no-one is waving back. H is on
a busted sofa, sinks so far in we have to pull her out. Then everyone reads their poetry
& it's like Central Market with the different languages, like Bowden's pavements
with their patterns of red bricks, like Linear Park with its riverrunsthroughit.
B calls us pilgrims of dust. J tweets bits of poems & someone in another
city, another country, reads them. T is fond of the crow's black
heart but his lungs are as light & white as angels & they fly
so tinydelicate from his mouth. Our hair is blond & brown & grey
& we ache in different ways & it is so fuckingbeautiful&sad
the way we all bear it. Someone says thank god for cut & paste. Hell
we all say it. It's life after all. D plays the soundtrack from Basquiat at the Barbican
& we're filled with it & we're boomforreal, ohyesweare. We are the idea
of Earth & the idea of earth. It's like the inside of an internal organ
the fleshy mess of LIFE that keeps on happening & happening even
if we close our eyes. We could be painted in oils, sitting along one side
of this long table with our beer & wine & food-truck burritos. Outside
there's the ping of trams shuttling Port Rd, their underground wires fizzing
& sparking & the labyrinth of dark streets, alleys, passageways
spidering their way through the whole city, away down to the beach
where allthewaterintheworld keeps breathing
in & out, regardless.

Versities: Building X
Peter Kirkpatrick

The places poetry takes you: resting,
not exactly on my laurels, by Building X
during a much-needed break in a creative
workshop – students are off getting coffee
or sit in twos and threes gossiping –
my mind, emblem-gathering,
drinks in an outer-suburban panorama
of sun-blanched paddocks that one time
yielded wine and, across the hill,
the ruins of a drive-in cinema.

But no signs arrive, beyond
the mass of Building X itself,
which was custom-built for Engineering,
with halls for important giant machines
secreted well away from the bland all-
purpose, flat-floor, AV-
enabled seminar room where I become,
in Comrade Stalin's charming phrase,
an engineer of human souls
– though he meant artist, I mean teacher.

This unit has proven a delight, despite
my reticence in modelling *how to*
when I myself still barely know;
when every costive effort comes about
by good chance, gameplay and revision.
And revision. It didn't click that *writing*
might become a conversation, though years
in front of black-now-whiteboards
has instilled the lesson that the happiest, best
teaching is. That the rest is lecturing.

Beyond its backward-facing craft,
its joinery, I can't tell anyone how poetry
is done. This, for instance, happens
to be an exercise in a relaxed
accentual four and sometimes five-

stressed, mostly unornamented line.
But you'd hardly know, as intonation
plays against projected beats,
and even when it smooths into pentameter,
rhythm depends on spoken emphasis.
And why in ten line stanzas?

As for content, that's best left to risk
and opportunity – like running a new class.
There's little art in talking pedagogy;
or nothing like the homeschooled homilies
or bloated speech balloons that hover
above *Creative Writing*. And I'm
no Horace, no Alexander Pope,
or erstwhile-edgy US professor
primed to write an *ars poetica* in verse
to make my case. I don't have a line.

Meanwhile, I'm still slacking off
by Building X's red brick. Around me,
these yellow-green ex-pastoral hills
reveal no symbols; and the abandoned drive-in,
its screen long gone, hasn't shown a film
in yonks. This is the thin end of the city
and I love it here more than I can say,
among young Outer Westerners
who come with hope and few assumptions,
and whose thinking is both sensuous and shy.

More than once, maybe deliberating
poets I disdain – Shelley or Wilfred Owen –
something a student offered spoke
so deeply against my doubt that I felt
the heavy weight of hours lift,
and a sudden drawing up of blinds:
moments so intense I blinked back tears.
You don't get that in other occupations.
Here's thanks, then, for the quirky,
unpredictive chemistry of teaching,

of never feeling wholly in control
but going with what's gifted by
each instant and its human elements –
not so unlike the games and guesswork
that make poems: those conversations
with the dialects we share. Speaking
of which, it's time now I returned
to *Seven Centuries of Poetry in English*
and to modelling – maybe imagery, maybe
an exercise in the discursive mode.

As the coffee-drinkers and the gossips
are gathered up to reinhabit
our small sub-set of Engineering,
I remind myself there are no metaphors
in nature; that the lost vineyards, the forsaken
drive-in, are only what we make of them.
In poems, x can equal y anytime. So,
as air-con chills the sunlight's semillon
and the AV-screen descends and brightens,
right here, right now, let y mark the spot.

The Reservoir
Mark Tredinnick

The waters of the lake lie wide awake and worry
                            the wind at dusk; like the feathers
Of the wood duck, they fret a rising easterly, which deepens their brown
To grey. These are captured waters, backed up behind the weir;
                                   they spread across the flats, and I sit beside them
As if beside my self, (*all by my own*, as my daughter said
                                          when she was young), and wonder where
The past has been, and I've been, all these passing
Years, pent up here this feathered moment at the close of day.

I've come to the reservoir to be among kin,
                          to sit and forget myself in birdsong. I've come
To the reservoir to sink: my hope is to slide from a mind
Shrill with hopeless schemes
                to put right everything that cannot be. I've had to let a life go,
Which had taken a lifetime to catch, and it helps
                                    to watch the kingfishers tie their flies
And wait. Hope is their knack, and I'd like to catch it again if I could.
My life is a clearing in the present moment's wood.
                             I live a holding pattern, currently,

Circling the days that were and the years
                              that might yet be, till I spy my soul again
And put down. I'm a migratory bird on its first run home,
No idea when this fetch will end
                    and far from any hint of land.
I'm finding my way by taking it,
                    finding my courage by losing it, like feathers in a storm.
I'm flying on faith and prospect and memories made new.
Between lives I've come back to a place that practises staying by changing

Every moment further back into itself.
                            When I had a family, I came here
To be alone; alone now, I come for the company; I offer myself up
                                    to the family of things.
I sit and wait for my self to arrive—or to rise, whichever wants to happen
First. I come to host myself home.
                        To remember all the rest of me I put by
Getting by, as it seems one must. Come now, friend; I think I can
                                  remember how you go.
Sit with me by the rez, and tell me where you've been
                        and what you've lost and loved and seen.

The water's a slate, neither clear nor clean,
                        and we can write here what we will, we can sketch
Some kind of future, or nothing much at all. Let us speak of children
And be sung again by water, swum again by fish and fished by herons,
                      our syntax remade in weed and reed and crab and mud and eel.
Let's find our way out by feel; let's carp and cry and wallow
For a bit, and smoke as many Marlboros as we please.
It's so thick, the water here, we might as well walk on it
                            while we talk of it, you and I.

The waters of the lake can hold us, you see,
                           when earth, itself, refutes our feet.
Or we can sink in it—this reservoir—all the way down
To the bowels of our grief. Seems nothing much will prosper till we do.
The waters of the lake are a mind
                                 without a memory: no reflections
Trouble the surface here, the way evening begins
To trouble the sky. A pelican walks the surface now
                                   like resilience and miracle and flies,

Heavier than hope, more elegant than plainsong,
                           for the coast. Blackbird rings
The night's alarm, and the waters of the lake grow dark and shine with
Everything one's life might be—
                         now that what you thought it was, that life,
Has lost its fight for ordinary air and sunk from sight, to find
New feet where only all the rest of who you always were
Can lead you in the dark, and swim the drowning
                             children of your past back up into the last
             of daylight's arms.

Note

Family of things. Mary Oliver, "Wild Geese"

Prepping for the Apocalypse (A Poet's Manual)

Robert H. F. Carver

I. Proem

This is where things get serious—the light
lying in heaps: raw umber, burnt sienna.
Autumn already and everything half done.

But after the courts and bells—the sentences
spoken in lofty places—you find yourself
shy for the first time in the company of words.

There are moments when you remember what it is
to be a leaper of cathedrals—to know
the secret rage of aphids; when all this seems
less than you bargained for.
                      You'd be content
to win back just a little of that brightness—
just a splinter ...
                But for now, you gather leaves
almost at random:
                'No, I never meant
to be a mender of icons, never sought
for reasons.'
              'Tell me: Who has seen us here?
The spice-box has our memory, the oat
purrs in the saucepan, and the field-mice grin,
nervous as un-danced schoolgirls.'
                    'Orlando in
a moonscape of cicadas—his lost wits
heaped up around him. Or some smiling child
trying to fix cut grass.'
                One day you'll return
To the old verities: rain on an iron roof.
A steel trunk full of rivets. Shoe-lasts. Anvils.
A stump-jump plough. The certainty of soup-tins.

One day, perhaps. But not yet ...

II. Street

At the end, there is always a street, blocked off
by women in scarf-helmets, banging saucepans
with butchers' arms.
                       Hell's first highway has
no other exit. All the mild misdeeds
you thought forgotten; all that you fibbed or filched;
the words you wrote—or didn't—the colloquies
(or casuistries) of skin—everything's
remembered.
                    Will they beat you? No. You'll pass
white-buttocked down the line; jostled, perhaps—
that's all—ears flaming, watching the steep road
for pot-holes, till their din fades and becomes
a thing half longed for.

III. Climb

Not far to go now—a dozen easy pieces
of foot- and finger-work should do the trick.
The soil is light but there is plenty to grip
(samphire or spinifex—you don't distinguish).

Already you see a version of yourself
striding across savannahs—or hacking creepers
succulent enough to swallow cities.

But before you know it, there is only air to climb.
The plateau of your thoughts is a nervous ridge
on which you pivot, drinking in the scene
served up before you: rocks and islets flung
from a madman's fist—and down there, on the beach,
tracks in the sand; a gull or two; the crisp
rind of the boat you burned.

IV. Biopsy

Your prayers are not enough. Your pale, white, hands—
puffed as a spider's egg-sac—fail to grip.
Where is your scepsis now? Strange how bright steel
can whet belief.
                But you must learn to move
not as the angels—light as lace-wings—but
wombat-wise, clumsy and loveable.

You may talk with the logicians—point to all
your quiddities and kumquats, heaped along
the raked edge of the evening. But do not trust
their ætiologies.
                Rather, draw them in
with pictures. Say, 'A dugong in a gown
danced with a lady, cheek to whisker.'
                              Lead them
up to the high room where the green ideas
sleep furiously and no one dares to wake them.

V. FUBAR

Tell it as it is, not as you'd
like it to be: the here, the now's fucked up
utterly—beyond all possible
repair. The spindle's busted; a wild bloom
of rust eats into everything; the cogs
slumber in silt.
                Shit happens. Or so they tell me.
That would be something—movement at least. But this
is costive. The moment squats. The future hunkers.
Nothing is born.
              Of course, there's still a chance:
Fix that connection. Mend that fuse. The switch
rocks in its cradle. One spark—half a spark—
could save us. The last tool left in the box
is hope.
      'Fail and we're fucked', you say.
                            Perhaps.
But if we fail, we'll do it royally:
Fucked up. Fucked out. Fucked into some wild blue yonder.

A Poem Containing Violence
Joan Fleming

This world is not conclusion
～ Emily Dickinson

Secret lakes all licked dry by the sun and the general preference of the Tanami desert for parch   all lakes but this one

look karkarra side   look those babies!

little ducklings
    cruising the shallows

though cruising implies   leisure
              in fact they are paddling for their lives

in
    we wade

the very air joystocked with exclamations
this countrywoman   hard hunter   her face lit   she cradles the fledging
                  aw   white stripelets and down

"but we leave it here mayi?   I say

the sun setting
the mud drying hard

"are we taking it --?
"but what will we --?
              the Toyota crammed with blankets mangere chickenbones
crowbars
          chip packets spilled food   dogs
      into the squash goes the duckling

aw little duckling   little mess
and I never see it again

The sure infiltrations of buffel grass
The feral cat of the plant world
The trample of camels   and the camels culled
        culled by the hundreds of thousands from helicopters by off-season kitchenhands with machine guns
    and
            lawa, we don't kill those camels   *they made the roads*

The preference I have for feeding only the glossiest dogs
the dogs with names   *Brownie   Honey   Max*
And not the unclaimed camp mongrels in their extravagant ugliness
                their hides more scab than fur

The fat and thin paper work for the dole
The seventy years of gaslit *No*'s
The obscurantisms and absurdities
      "I understand your concerns about the penalty however the scheme requires you to attend your designated
      "no I'm sorry funeral leave has not been documented in your Centrelink portal as far as I can see on my screen here however if you'd like to fill out this form

The lack of native species featured on the print of children's pyjamas available for purchase on the racks of Australian family chain stores i.e. Kmart
        and the grief of the Conservation Minister at this fact
           O where will the Conservation Minister find bilby pyjamas for his children?

The way I ponder the duckling
and circle words like "casual   and "cruelty
while cruising the Kuala Lumpur markets for bargain leathergoods
chewing on a chicken skewer

"I'll need your date of birth please

"I'm sorry but that doesn't appear to be your date of birth

"Are there any other dates of birth that may be documented on the system

"I'm sorry but I cannot action your payment of the phone bill until we can locate you on the system through means of your date of birth

The pleasing curve of the ribs of the bullock
we call it 'killer'   in its cloth bag

The churr of tyres as we hoon the subtle desertscape   the cab suffused with
honest hot gun oil stink   bang / bang / bang /
the limpness of the turkey's head when I pluck it
the darkmeat supper so good behind the wheel   soul skipping only a little on
the CD, driving, sunset   even better with chickensalt

The husband's Hello back at camp   drumbellied and sipping on a bored smoke
          did she shoot anything?   (well, yeah   but we ate it)

  The new white relief couple who've run outback stores *in some really*
  nice places you know   yeah   nice up in the gulf good fishing
  (and what about the people)
   well they're the same everywhere aren't they you know what it's like
like "they" is a fruit tending brown   a bitter taste
   a fruit with a smell on it

The shame flip in my own pale gut my
culturally particular revulsions:
        a mother picking nits and crunching them
        a child playing with the hairbrush clumps and offering them
        a wife lifting the lung from the cooking wire
                and tearing off a strip
                and giving it a red squeeze

The friend of my uncle the ragged boast of his felt hat
his joke his rattling laugh behind the wheel of the bush bus
The only animals that can talk

The son first blurring the car towards the easternmost post of his mother's house
    and ramming
then blurring the car towards the westernmost post
which faces the sorry camps and the red plateau un-seeable in the dark but for
how it blocks
    the stars
    and ramming

The son who turns the knife and turns the knife and turns it
and his red stomach

The grog
The sweet sugar everywhere grog   relentless partial foaming wreckage
its seethe, its loosening

My auntie and uncle grew me up they was always fighting
when you grow up like that in a couple years you fighting too
I got big in jail "Like, strong? *no, fat haha*
"Why were you in jail? *I was hitting my missus but I didn't know that little baby was coming*

The comparing of scars
I got this scar when I tore my meniscus doing party dancing   I say
This scar, look   she says   when my first husband been bossing me
stab me in the knee

The gathering up of emu feathers in the thin morning
I've never run my whorls up a quill so silk

nor felt so stifled bored
I ever cut the chicken wire and finished   a pair of emu

The feathers and their carrying-away
The darkmeat taste and its carrying-away
            and the easy image carried away
            and my walk-away private white mind

About the Newcastle Poetry Prize

The Newcastle Poetry Prize is a significant cultural achievement and is a testament to the commitment of its sponsor - the University of Newcastle – to celebrate literary excellence in Australian poetry.

In September 1980, Peter Goldman stood in the middle of Civic Park, Newcastle, during the Mattara Festival and handed out an A4 photocopied anthology of poetry to passers-by. The collection featured poems from local Hunter writers, with contributors ranging in age from six to eighty-one. This humble anthology paved the way for the first official Mattara Poetry Prize in 1981, which has gone on to become the most prestigious poetry competition in the country, and is now known as the Newcastle Poetry Prize.

Today the Newcastle Poetry Prize is one of the major events on the literary calender in Australia, bringing entries from across the nation. Each year, local and national poets compete with internationally recognised names and no less illustrious has been the list of judges casting their eye over the entries. These include Christopher Pollintz, Peter Porter, Chris Wallace-Crabbe, Paul Kavanagh, Les Murray, Dame Leonie Kramer, Fay Zwicky, Dorothy Hewett, Antigone Kefala, Robert Gray, Kim Cheng-Boey, Jean Kent, Dennis Haskell, Mark Tredinnick and Judith Beveridge.

The association with Newcastle is no accident. The Hunter Region has a long history of fostering poetry and an active community of local poets who punch above their weight nationally in awards, publication and events. In the words of the late Novocastrian poet, Bill Iden, "Newcastle's environment makes its poets".

Co-ordinated by Hunter Writers Centre (a not-for-profit organisation since 1995), the Newcastle Poetry Prize is one of Australia's oldest and most important literary competitions in Australia. This is made possible through the generous provision of the prize money by the University of Newcastle and through funding from Create NSW

Harri Jones Memorial Prize

Thomas Henry (Harri) Jones was born in a remote area of Wales in 1921, the eldest of five children and the only son in a poor rural family. He won scholarships to secondary school in Builth Wells and then to university in Aberystwyth. His studies were interrupted by World War II when he served in the Navy. He met his wife, Madeleine, when they were demobbed after the war. After completing his Master's degree in the post-war years, he taught English to returned servicemen at the Naval Dockyards in Portsmouth, England. He and Madeleine moved to Newcastle NSW in 1959 with their three young daughters. Harri had obtained a lectureship in the Department of English of the then University College of Newcastle, an offshoot of the University of New South Wales. This was meant to be a short-term move, with the hope of returning to Britain when Harri secured a lectureship there.

Harri is a well-known Anglo-Welsh poet and in addition to his books of poetry he is well represented in anthologies of poetry in Australia and elsewhere. He published his first volume of poetry in 1957. His fourth and last was published posthumously in 1966. He was very well regarded as a lecturer despite the alcoholism that marred his latter years and ended with his untimely death by drowning in 1965 at the age of 43. After his death, family and friends donated money in his memory to set up a poetry prize to continue in perpetuity. Harri had a significant impact on his students, several of whom went on to fine careers of their own as writers and academics.

www.ingramcontent.com/pod-product-compliance
Lightning Source LLC
LaVergne TN
LVHW051524070426
835507LV00023B/3296